# Praise for *Abandoned Faith*

As someone whose life work is to strengthen the faith of millennials, I see this book as a caring guide chock-full of practical advice. As a dad of millennials, I see it as a well-timed life preserver in the swelling waves of a cultural storm.

**JEFF MYERS, PHD**
President, Summit Ministries
Author of *Understanding the Culture*

I have had the privilege of knowing Jason for many years. His ministry is on the front line for today's student. *Abandoned Faith* from Focus on the Family is a timely tool for all of us concerned about reaching people under the age of 25. You'll find insight and help from Jason and Alex's message in this book. If you're like me, once you start reading, you won't be able to put it down!

**DR. SCOTT DAWSON**
Founder and President, Scott Dawson Evangelistic Association
Director, AtlantaFest and Stadium Fest

As a father and a pastor, I appreciate both the honesty with which Jason and Alex present the current situation of many of our millennials and also the hope they offer. This book is full of Scripture, statistics, and an abundance of practical ideas to help the millennial in your life.

**ALEX KENNEDY**
Senior Pastor, Carmel Baptist Church

D0775991

If you're like me, you're aware of the problem: young Christians often walk away from the Church in their high-school and college years. Jason Jimenez and Alex McFarland have written *Abandoned Faith* in an effort to do something about it. They've been working with millennials for years, and they've written a resource to help the Church appreciate the challenge, understand the nature of those who are leaving, and begin to consider an effective response. *Abandoned Faith* is an important book. It will help you understand what is at stake and what you can do about it.

J. WARNER WALLACE
Cold-Case Detective, Adjunct Professor of Apologetics at Biola University
Author of *Cold-Case Christianity*, *Cold-Case Christianity for Kids*, and *God's Crime Scene*

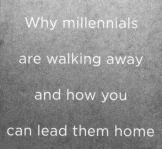

Why millennials
are walking away
and how you
can lead them home

# ABANDONED
# FAITH

## ALEX McFARLAND

## JASON JIMENEZ

TYNDALE HOUSE PUBLISHERS, INC.
CAROL STREAM, ILLINOIS

*Abandoned Faith: Why Millennials Are Walking Away and How You Can Lead Them Home*
© 2017 Alex McFarland and Jason Jimenez. All rights reserved.

A Focus on the Family book published by Tyndale House Publishers, Inc., Carol Stream, Illinois 60188

*Focus on the Family* and the accompanying logo and design are federally registered trademarks of Focus on the Family, 8605 Explorer Drive, Colorado Springs, CO 80920.

*TYNDALE* and Tyndale's quill logo are registered trademarks of Tyndale House Publishers, Inc.

Editor: Liz Duckworth
Cover design by Julie Chen

Cover photograph copyright © Pearl/Lightstock. All rights reserved.

For information about special discounts for bulk purchases, please contact Tyndale House Publishers at csresponse@tyndale.com or call 800-323-9400.

**Library of Congress Cataloging-in-Publication Data**
Names: McFarland, Alex, 1964- author. | Jimenez, Jason, 1979- author.
Title: Abandoned faith : why millennials are walking away and how you can lead them home / Alex McFarland and Jason Jimenez.
Description: Carol Stream, Illinois : Tyndale House Publishers, Inc., [2017] | Includes bibliographical references.
Identifiers: LCCN 2016047375 | ISBN 9781589978829 (alk. paper)
Subjects: LCSH: Generation Y--Religious life. | Ex-church members. | Non-church-affiliated people. | Parent and adult child—Religious aspects—Christianity.
Classification: LCC BV4529.2 .M38 2017 | DDC 248.8/45—dc23
LC record available at https://urldefense.proofpoint.com/v2/url?u=https-3A__lccn.loc.gov_2016047375&d=DgIF-g&c=6BNjZEuL_DAs869UxGis0g&r=RiCinEsc4dq ZkJzwU5MYFNAvmTxtQhRNGR9VDw0v6kQ&m=zNak27e9Uq3qWWdyn IKLURy5uAjomnrk6VOUMdNIk3c&s=DuGCHc-Y6268HTt0ugx6bPCZloxey SgNvXVh_dxXD5g&e=

Printed in the United States of America

23  22  21  20  19  18  17
7   6   5   4   3   2   1

# Contents

Foreword by Sean McDowell  *vii*

INTRODUCTION: From Christianity to Atheism  *ix*

PART ONE: **What Went Wrong?**

1. Hope for Hurting Parents  *3*
2. Why Millennials Are Leaving the Faith  *23*
3. What Lies Behind Abandoned Faith?  *55*
4. How the Church Is Failing Millennials (and How It Can Improve)  *69*

PART TWO: **Forces Shaping Our Sons and Daughters**

5. Struggles Millennials Face  *91*
6. Understanding What Drives Millennials  *107*
7. Hope for a Generation  *119*

PART THREE: **Steps to Mend and Move Forward**

8. Strengthening Your Relationship in Stressful Times  *143*
9. Bridging the Gap  *155*

10. Helping Your Child Bounce Back
    from Tough Breaks *173*

PART FOUR: **Winning Back Your Millennial Child**
11. The Power of a Prayer Map *203*
12. Build a Foundation of Biblical
    Truth *221*

CONCLUSION: Jesus Is the Key *243*

APPENDIX: When There Is a Failure to Launch *251*
    Acknowledgments *259*
    Notes *261*
    About the Authors *267*

# Foreword

THERE HAS BEEN A lot of talk recently about why kids are leaving the church. Experts have rightly pointed out that the issue is complex and may involve a host of reasons—intellectual, volitional, personal, relational, spiritual, moral, and more. And yet amidst the difficulty of the matter (both personally and intellectually), my friends Alex McFarland and Jason Jimenez offer a timely book: *Abandoned Faith: Why Millennials are Walking Away and How You Can Lead Them Home.*

I have personally read dozens of excellent books aiming to identify why Christian young people are abandoning the church (and often their faith) in disquieting numbers, and how we can best respond. *Abandoned Faith* is now one of my favorite books. Allow me to briefly share four reasons why.

First, Alex and Jason work with millennials. This is not a solely academic book written from a distance. While there is undoubtedly value in purely scholastic research, this book is filled with personal stories from two authors who both know and love millennials. *Abandoned Faith* is not written from an outsider's perspective but from two experts who both "get" millennials.

Second, *Abandoned Faith* is research based. Alex and Jason have plenty of firsthand experiences with millennials. In fact, much of the book is filled with stories, which I love! But they also draw deeply from documented research about the thinking, behavior, and unique experience of millennials. They also draw from the expertise of other pastors, teachers, parents, and researchers who work with millennials. Alex and Jason have clearly done their homework.

Third, the book is hopeful. Right at the beginning, the authors recognize that some people reading *Abandoned Faith* might feel a sense of personal regret about the way they have interacted with millennials. In fact, there are probably many parents reading this book who wish they could have a parenting "do over." Yet rather than sending a message of guilt, Jason and Alex intentionally cover the book in God's grace. In fact, personally speaking, I found this to be one of the most powerful elements in the book.

Fourth, *Abandoned Faith* is practical. Since I am a professor, I do love research. But I also appreciate when people offer practical steps I can personally take to apply research to my own parenting, speaking, counseling, and ministry to young people. This is exactly what Jason and Alex do.

If you work with millennials in any capacity—such as parenting, pastoring, or even in some professional capacity—this book will be tremendously valuable to you. I am personally grateful that Alex and Jason have taken the time to both research and write this book. After reading it, I feel more motivated and equipped to reach millennials. May God use *Abandoned Faith* to both equip and motivate you in the same way.

*Sean McDowell, PhD*
Professor of apologetics at Biola University, internationally recognized speaker, and bestselling author of more than 15 books, including *A New Kind of Apologist*

# FROM CHRISTIANITY TO ATHEISM

THE FAMILY HAD GATHERED for Daniel's birthday party, the oldest son, who was about to turn 25. Daniel was excited to see his relatives, especially his youngest brother, Clayton, a second-semester sophomore attending college in another state.

Daniel had not seen Clayton in over a year.

Growing up in a Christian home, the brothers were close through the years. Daniel had been a spiritual mentor to his younger brother. They grew up praying together and attending Christian camp in the summer. Daniel was at Clayton's baptism when Clayton made a profession of faith as a teenager.

Shortly after the birthday meal blessing, conversation turned to Clayton and his studies as a sophomore. It came to light that classes taught by a professor who was part of The Jesus Seminar had influenced Clayton. (This group of liberal scholars is known for their rejection of the New Testament. Their research methods have been highly criticized and their conclusions against the Bible almost universally rejected, yet their detrimental influence in the lives of impressionable young students continues.)

Clayton shocked his family by announcing that he was now an atheist. When his uncle at the birthday party began to defend God and Christianity, Clayton quickly responded, "Uncle, are you aware that belief in the virgin birth of Christ was influenced by ancient paganism?"

Clayton's father explained what the Bible says about the virgin birth of Christ. He hoped years of raising his son in a Christian home and spending thousands of dollars on Christian education hadn't gone to waste.

Clayton, the newborn atheist, retorted, "Dad. I know you may not like this, but I don't believe in the Bible anymore. I've learned the Bible can't be trusted. The church has doctored it up through the centuries. It's all a lie."

Clayton's "coming out as an atheist" put a damper on Daniel's birthday party. The final straw was when the young man stated, "Don't worry, I am still religious. I worship Richard Dawkins."

This account (a true story) is all too similar to experiences in the lives of millions of twentysomethings and their families. We have heard it in many forms and all too often.

## Raised to Believe Nothing

Meeting with a college student over a cup of coffee, I (Jason) could see he was pretty shaken up. I sat back in my chair and asked the young man why he was so uneasy.

He collected his thoughts and replied, "I've really been struggling lately with what I've been raised to believe." He set his coffee down and sat up in his chair. "I know it's not entirely my parents' fault, but I don't think they did a very good job teaching me the Bible and demonstrating how a Christian should live."

Appreciating his candor, I said, "That may be the case. But rather than focus on the failures of your parents, are you open to figuring out what it is that you believe?"

Thankfully, he agreed.

After months of discipleship and meeting with the student's parents, it warms my heart to say the family is reconnected and continues to live boldly for Christ. This student's situation was similar to Clayton's, but it had a very different outcome. There is always hope.

## Image Problem

We have seen vast numbers of students like Clayton and have talked with their families. We have had thousands of discussions with millennials and their parents about family struggles, friendship concerns, and faith doubts. Our travels, conversations, and in-depth studies have helped us discover some unfortunate truths.

Despite the footprint of Christianity in America, its mark on millennials is not as visible as it was with previous generations. An older generation of Christians is dying off and the newer generation's influence is waning. This millennial generation consists of those born between roughly 1982 and 2004, though experts cannot agree on specific beginning and end dates. These are your sons and daughters, and their outlook on faith may be vastly different from your own.

*These are your sons and daughters, and their outlook on faith may be vastly different from your own.*

Over 80 percent of Christians (both young and old) are considered biblically illiterate. That means a mere 2 out of every 10 Christians know how to live, articulate, and defend the Christian faith. Woodrow Kroll commented, "When we speak of creeping Bible illiteracy in America, we are not talking about the inability to read but the choice not to read . . . This failure to read the Bible consistently, or to hear its truth consistently, is the major factor in Bible illiteracy in America. It is an epidemic in . . . America."[1]

Without learning and applying the fundamentals of the Christian faith, the hearts and minds of millions of young people have become less inclined to embrace Christianity. They have failed to become authentic followers of Jesus Christ.

Statistics show that roughly 70 percent of Americans identify themselves as Christian.[2] But when you examine the information a bit further, you find that most have a distorted version of Christianity. This speaks to the "image problem" we face in America. Most Americans view themselves as "Christians," but not many live the way a Christian is called to live. As a result, many young people reject what they believe to be Christianity, when in fact, they are really rejecting a false representation of it.

In their book *UnChristian*, David Kinnaman and Gabe Lyons write, "Our research shows that many of those outside of Christianity, especially younger adults, have little trust in the Christian faith, and esteem for the lifestyle of Christ followers is quickly fading among outsiders. They admit their emotional and intellectual barriers go up when they are around Christians, and they reject Jesus because they feel rejected by Christians."[3]

A growing number of millennials are unaffiliated with any particular religion. When asked to designate their religion from a list, most choose "none of the above." (This group has become widely known as the "nones.") Yet despite a lack of affiliation, it's surprising how often these young people pray and hunger for real answers.[4] It speaks to the desire of millennials to live authentic lives marked with credibility. The majority believe in significance and yearn to make a difference. There's just one problem: They don't know how to do it.

*A growing number of millennials are unaffiliated with any particular religion.*

So there is hope after all. And mom and dad, this is where you come in!

We don't believe we will win back the hearts and minds of this age of "nones" by overtly trying to make Christianity "attractive."

We believe it will take a miracle. Really.

But we have faith. We have faith that God will do such a miracle in the lives of our young people. We trust revival will break out in the midst of this generation. We believe the one child who abandoned the faith will once again stand strong for Christ.

The Scripture makes it clear it is incumbent upon all parents to teach and train their children in the timeless truths of the Bible (Deuteronomy 6; Psalm 78). Paul writes, "Follow the pattern of the sound words that you have heard from me, in the faith and love that are in Christ Jesus" (2 Timothy 1:13).

When parents strive to model a *pattern* of Christianity to their millennial children, those children are far more likely to follow in their parents' footsteps. There is no one more powerful and uniquely qualified to do this than mom and dad. There is nothing more compelling and persuasive than a parent living out his or her faith with great boldness and conviction.

**There is nothing more compelling and persuasive than a parent living out his or her faith.**

However, parents must be willing to step up and step out to assume their spiritual roles in the lives of their millennial children. The family is central to the spiritual formation of any child (regardless of the age); but if parents lack the passion and drive to live it and teach it, then the world will ultimately shape our children. (You don't want that, and neither do we.)

Ever since your child came into the world, you loved, comforted, fed, clothed, and instructed him or her. You can say that you did the best you could to meet your child's physical needs.

*But what about his or her spiritual needs?*

What did you and your spouse do to sharpen your millennial's biblical worldview? Is your adult child's faith stronger now than it was when he or she was a child? Whether or not your adult child is living for Christ, it's natural for a parent to feel some responsibility. On the other hand, some parents take all the blame for their adult child's sinful choices.

Many parents we talk to wish they could go back in time and undo the mistakes they made with their children.

One couple said that seeing their college-age child living in sin and professing atheism reminds them constantly of their failure to raise him in the truth and grace of Christ. When their son was growing up, dad traveled while mom did her best to raise the kids. They described their home as Christian, but after years of arguing and fighting, they realized how far they were from truly living a Christian life. We will never forget these words: "Every time we see our son fail, it reminds us of how we failed him."

*"Every time we see our son fail, it reminds us of how we failed him."*

We are here not to blame parents like these for past failures but to help them understand contributing factors in their adult children's lives and move forward with hope for their adult children.

## We're Losing Altitude!

In a recent study, LifeWay Research and Fuller Youth Institute estimated that over half of high school graduates will leave the church and become disengaged in their faith. This is alarming because many emerging adults are making big decisions that affect more than just their own lives—and they are making those decisions without faith in God.

You may have a child who has rejected Christianity, or you may simply have a desire to help build an unshakable foundation for your child. Whatever the case, Christian parents need to be armed and ready to wage war for the hearts and souls of their adult children.

*We are knee-deep in a culture war for our children's faith.*

We are knee-deep in a culture war for our children's faith and for the future fate of Christianity in America. Satan never stops scheming and spreading lies. He doesn't want you standing firm in the faith, nor does he want you leading your family. He uses the guilt and regret many parents carry to advance his agenda.

It's clearly going to take a lot of prayer and hard work to equip parents to rise up and use their influence and faith to change the direction of their homes.

But it's worth it.

If you're desperate to learn about your millennial and you want to find a better and more powerful way to communicate with him or her, then we welcome this opportunity to help reinforce your responsibility to have a strong relationship with your adult child.

Your child might be an adult, but that doesn't mean you're not to play a role in his or her life. We want to empower you to do that, so we've sought some of the most respected Christian minds to help you understand the worldview of typical millennials and, hopefully, to bridge the gaps that exist between you and your adult child.

It is our prayer that each page will deepen your faith and equip you with the courage you need to become the parent your children (young or old) need you to be.

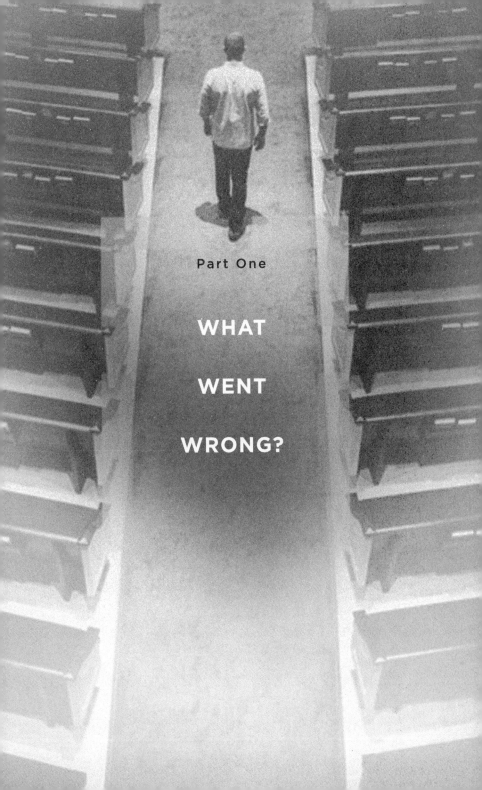

Part One

# WHAT

# WENT

# WRONG?

# Chapter 1

# HOPE FOR HURTING PARENTS

IN AN AUDIENCE OF 200 ADULTS, I (Jason) asked, "Does anyone here have a son or daughter who has left the faith?" The response was startling. Almost every couple in the room had a child who had left the faith.

In one sense, as the different couples raised their hands, there was a sense of relief in the group. Parents realized that they weren't the only ones whose children had "wandered." It was moving to see these parents share so openly. It also was powerful evidence of the size of the problem.

One older gentleman said, "My son didn't want anything to do with God after his mother died." Another woman said, "My daughter came out as a lesbian. And when she did, the church didn't want anything to do with her. This was the church she grew up in. But because the rejection she received was so harsh, it caused her to doubt everything she believed growing up."

To my surprise, the stories kept coming. I had planned to teach an entire lesson, but the Holy Spirit had other plans. After hearing such deep-seated pain from so many in the class, I stood before them in silence. Before I could say anything, the sound of sobbing came from a well-dressed man in the back. He was sitting next to his wife, with their hands clinched together. She was tearful as well. I motioned to him, trying to offer some comfort. He raised his head, attempting to gain control, as the group listened in anticipation.

Finding strength, the father finally said, "I didn't do enough." The moment he said that, his wife grabbed his hand and tightly brought it to her chest. He quickly sank into his chair and placed his head in his open hands. I gave him some time, then asked what he meant by saying he didn't do enough.

He sat up. "I wasn't there for my kids the way I needed to be as a father. And now they're grown up, and neither of them has a strong faith. I should've done more. I should've been more of a leader, rather than leave my wife or the church to do it for me."

After the meeting, I spoke with the wife of this man. He was probably too emotional to stick around. She shared a few additional things about her adult children and explained how she and her husband were slowly working through the pain. I reassured her about her position in Christ and her influential role as a mother.

After gathering my things, I walked out of the room with a man who had several grandchildren. He expressed how much the class meant to him. I put my arm around him, and thanked him for being so kind. He then stopped and said, "You know that man who shared he wished he'd spent more time discipling his kids?"

I nodded.

He said, "I not only wish I did more for my kids, but now, at my age, I also have grandkids who are not living for the Lord. That pains me more than anything. And I feel I contributed to that, like a generational curse. I didn't really live out my faith. It was more like something I kept to myself. And now, my kids and their kids aren't living for Jesus."

*The feelings of regret were so strong among that group of parents.*

The feelings of regret were so strong among that group of parents. Their pain was shared and common in the large audience. It may be pain you feel yourself—one accompanied by a sense of hopelessness. Take heart. You are not alone.

## Christian Parents and Their Millennial Children

God's design for family is for parents to raise their children in the fear and admonition of the Lord—to train them to live holy lives. Proverbs 14:27 says, "The fear of the LORD is a fountain of life, that one may turn away from the snares of death." Though this proverb is true and worthy of all acceptance, it is not an easy one to follow consistently. It would have been great if you (as the parent) had told your kids to fear God and follow your picture-perfect example. If they did, they would escape death and receive the fountain of life.

But that's not usually how it works out.

The truth is, most parents try to raise their children in the fear of the Lord. Unfortunately, many of these children (now adults) still turn away from Christianity. The purpose of this book is to help you understand what has happened generationally and discover how you can respond in a positive way.

*Many have sought answers to explain the decline of Christianity among millennials.*

The shift in faith on the part of the millennial generation has captured the minds of experts and produced a ton of research. From the psychologists to student pastors, many have sought answers to explain the decline of Christianity among millennials.

*What happened to them?*

*Why are millennials leaving the church?*

*Where did we go wrong?*

*Will they ever come back?*

These, and many other questions, have plagued the hearts and minds of loved ones—mostly parents.

Much focus in the church these days has been directed

at reaching twentysomethings. So far, the church has been generally unsuccessful.

Attempts to "dumb down" the message of the gospel have been a big mistake.

There have been efforts to modernize and introduce loud, secularized worship music, played by people on stage wearing beanies, tight cut V-neck T-shirts, and ridiculously skinny jeans. Fail.

Some churches have attempted to create an atmosphere where everyone is right and no one is wrong. Total fail.

Many of these attempts to *reach* millennials have not worked. We are not surprised. After a combined 40 years of working with millennials, we can tell you that much of the church's strategy is totally wrong.

Ministering to millennials is a daunting task. You never know what you are going to get from them. Especially from embittered ones raised in so-called "Christian" homes. Yet despite the massive decline of Christianity among millennials (which we will examine in depth), we are seeing many of them return to Christ, like the Prodigal Son described in Luke 15.

*Ministering to millennials is a daunting task.*

Our point is, there is still hope. No matter what you are going through right now with your son or daughter—know that there is still hope. Hope for you, your spouse, and your child. But if you and your spouse want to receive hope and healing, then you first need to face your pain, your regrets, and your fears and doubts.

Let's address these difficult issues together, one by one.

## Unspeakable Pain

Church pews are filled with parents experiencing deep pain—pain over the fact that their son or daughter (or both) is no longer living for Christ.

Most parents, if they are honest, will tell you they are hurting. They hurt over the bad choices their adult children are making. They hurt over the intimacy they once had with their son or daughter.

Sunday after Sunday, parents sit in church, then go off to their Sunday school classes never speaking of the pain they suffer over their millennial child. And if they do share about this pain, it's often presented as a silent prayer request and nothing more.

This silent suffering has to stop.

Often we are so worried about the spiritual state of millennials that we have neglected to care for the condition of their parents. The amount of pain experienced by parents is overwhelming. They are getting hammered. Consider this email from a mother about her son:

> When your children are younger, it is so much easier
> to involve yourself in their lives. But when they
> get older and leave home, it's much more difficult
> to know your place. When your child pushes you
> away and makes his own bad decisions and then
> wants your help, only to disregard it again, it breaks
> your heart. As a parent, instead of looking forward

to talking with your adult children, you begin to dread the calls because you know that there will be another issue to deal with. You want to be the hero and have all the answers. But you know that no matter what you say, they won't always listen. It's a tough place to be in because you feel disrespected, and angry—and on top of it all, you feel like you failed your child. All I want is to have a mature and healthy relationship with them. All I want is for my children to need me in their lives.

*If we are going to win millennials back to Christ, we first need to win parents back to hope and healing.*

What a moving message. The heart of this mother captures what many parents feel.

It's too easy to overlook the pain of parents when all the attention is on the problems of their children. Yet, if we are going to win millennials back to Christ, we first need to win parents back to hope and healing.

Unfortunately, many of the problems millennials deal with stem from their parents. Whether these are problems of divorce, hypocrisy, dysfunctional relationships, legalism, overprotective parenting—whatever the case—if we are going to see a major turnaround among millennials, they need to see change first in moms and dads.

We have had many conversations with millennials on this very topic. Many have said that although they were raised in Christian homes, it never seemed Christianity was at the core of everything they did. I (Jason) remember one college student saying, "I think the only reason my parents go to church is to feel better about themselves."

Another student said, "The only time we learned about the Bible was when we went to church."

That's not to say these parents didn't try or didn't care. Not at all. What millennials are saying is that the gospel was not at the center of their homes. It was a part of home life, but it was not the totality of it. The transfer of the Christian faith from one generation (parents) to the next (their children) is almost nonexistent. Millennials may have received a degree of faith from a parent or parents, but it wasn't enough for them to see the value and importance faith has in their own lives.

This is a painful reality for parents. It's painful because their millennials are right. In too many families, faith went only as far as church attendance. Sure, throw in a few extra church activities, a few family devotions, and lectures about doing the right thing. But the truth is, many parents do feel they failed in leading their children spiritually. Now that their kids are adults, these same parents struggle with relating to them. All they can do is watch helplessly as their adult children live their lives not for God but for themselves.

## Waves of Regret

As parents open up about this deep pain, inevitably a great deal of regret resides within each one. These parents have tried everything to get rid of it, but the regret never seems to go away.

I (Jason) remember an older pastor sharing with me about his prodigal son. He and I were sitting in his office before I was about to preach in his church. I saw many pictures of his beautiful family there. But I noticed he had current pictures only of his daughters and not his son. When I commented on it, he said that he and his wife had not spoken to their son in years.

The pastor teared up and said, "I'm to blame that he's running away from God. I was too busy ministering to others, and I didn't do enough for my son. That's my biggest regret."

Sound familiar? Take out *ministering to others* and fill in the blank. The fact is, there is not one single parent alive in this world free from regret. We all have regrets and know other godly parents who do as well.

*We all have regrets and know other godly parents who do as well.*

Sean Lee is a caring and vibrant woman who has served as a children's director for nearly thirty years. She is well respected and does an outstanding job ministering to children and families.

When I (Jason) asked her about parental regrets, Sean said she wished she had done a better job helping her three boys engage the culture, especially when they were in high school. "Instead of engaging them in conversation about cultural issues, I was more concerned with trying to protect them. My husband and I were constantly evaluating their choices, especially in terms of their friends. We would freak out if they were around things we were trying so hard to protect them from. By the time they went off to college, it was a real culture shock for our boys. Looking back now, I wish we hadn't sheltered them so much but instead rephrased a lot of the conversation with them so they were more prepared when they went to college."

Sean acknowledged that many parents feel the same way she does. But rather than sulk about it, Sean said she has learned from her mistakes and works hard to maintain healthy and strong relationships with each of her boys.

We need to let our regrets go just as Sean did. She knew that if she was going to continue to impact her boys in their adult years, she had to learn what they needed from her. She would need to be a support to them whenever and however it was required, to listen when they needed to talk, and to be there to ask penetrating questions as they thought through their decisions.

Sean learned about God's grace in the hard times of parenting. "Parenting is about grace. My parenting may never be perfect, but when I seek God's grace day after day, I actually have learned more about His love for me and what I am truly capable of accomplishing as a mother."

In her book *Building the Christian Family You Never Had,* Mary DeMuth spoke of letting go of regret: "Inevitably we carry some amount of parental regret. Freedom from regret comes when we admit our weaknesses before Jesus. No one is perfect. Our imperfections, though, shouldn't become a wall between God and us or our children and God. At the cross we can lay down our regrets over our failures and move on. Remember that even the great heroes of the Bible did things they regretted."[1]

*Holding on to regrets prevents you from experiencing true freedom in Christ.*

Holding on to regrets prevents you from experiencing true freedom in Christ. It's hard not to think back on all the moments you should have acted differently. Every time you recall those not-so-fond moments with your adult child, the less happiness and joy you will feel.

Being tossed around by waves of regret is actually where Satan, the great Adversary, wants you to be. He doesn't want you to let your regrets go. He wants you to drown in them. Every time you see your son or daughter making bad choices, Satan wants you to feel regret. He wants you to blame yourself for their sinful choices. But like the apostle Paul, you need to gain this assurance: "One thing I do: forgetting what lies behind and straining forward to what lies ahead" (Philippians 3:13).

A *woulda-coulda-shoulda* attitude does not help you. It only makes matters worse between you and your millennial child. The key is not to *regret* having regrets. (That only brings on more regrets.) Instead, give your regrets over to God and allow His healing power to take control of your life. As the old saying goes: *you can't change the past, but you can learn from it.*

In addition to pain and regret, there is a dual enemy we must also confront—fear and doubt.

## Enabling Fear and Doubt

Raising kids is scary. Especially when you have to let them go. When they were younger, you were there for them, 24/7. You made decisions for them because they were too young to make decisions for themselves. Now they are all grown up, and you have to trust that everything you taught them won't be forgotten. Of course, children (young or old) won't always do the right thing. They will make mistakes, mistakes you cannot (or should not) fix. It's a touchy subject, especially for enabler parents who tend to interfere with all aspects of a child's life.

Let's put this into perspective by way of a story about a desperate mother.

We were filling in as speakers on a radio show that was about to wrap up. On the incoming-calls screen was this question from a caller: *How can I win back my daughter to Christ?*

We immediately grabbed the call, knowing that we didn't have much time. We welcomed the caller to the show and asked how we could be of help. She immediately began to cry on the air. After a long pause (which is very awkward on radio), she gained her composure. She had just gotten into another argument with her daughter. They had both lost it, and the mother had gotten into the car and taken off.

Her radio was tuned to our program, and she heard what we were talking about and called in. We were glad she did.

The mother explained that she tried to raise her daughter in a Christian home. But the daughter rejected everything the mother stood for. She tried everything, but nothing reached the young woman.

Our hearts broke for this mother. And for her daughter.

With limited time, I (Jason) began to ask this mother a series of questions. It turned out the woman was divorced, an overprotective parent who always *fixed* her daughter's mistakes. Naturally, there was a lot of resentment between mom and daughter, and it was obvious that good communication wasn't a skill either possessed.

**"Why won't you stop trying to fix your daughter, and let God fix you?"**

After hearing the discouragement in this mother's voice, I asked one final question: "Why won't you stop trying to fix your daughter, and let God fix you?"

There was dead silence. We thought we had lost her. But then the mother answered, "Because I'm too afraid."

Wow. What a response. What honesty. This mother expressed what a lot of moms are feeling. For this mom to really be a help to her daughter, she first needed to seek God's help in her own life.

Too often, as parents, we think we know what's best for our kids when, really, God knows best. We love our children, but God loves them so much more. We believe we know our children better than anyone, yet God knew them before they were born. We are assured in Psalm 139:16, "Your eyes saw my unformed substance; in your book were written, every one of them, the days that were formed for me, when as yet there was none of them."

As parents, we can become so overly protective that we neglect to lean into God's protection for our children. Like this desperate mother on the radio, parents try to do most of the heavy lifting for their millennial children. There is no denying the love and desires parents have for their children. But stepping in to fix everything isn't healthy.

Now, parental enablers will argue that they do what they do because their children are incapable of doing it themselves. That may be true to some extent. But the truth is, enabling parents do what they do out of fear. They fear their children will get hurt, or they believe their kids *can't* do anything without them. And some fear they will not be needed anymore.

Allison Bottke, bestselling author of the acclaimed *Setting Boundaries* series, writes, "Our biggest problem isn't about our adult child's inability to wake up when his alarm clock rings, or her inability to keep a schedule, hold down a job, or pay the bills. It's not about drug use or alcohol addictions. It's not about the mess these adult children are making of their life. The main problem is about the part we're playing in stepping in to soften the blow of the consequences that come from the choices they make. *The main problem is us.*"[2]

*Out of fear, some parents never adjust their level of attachment in their kids' lives, as they get older.*

Too often we pick on a grown-up child for being lazy or too dependent on mom or dad. In reality, the actual problem *might just be* mom and dad. This *fear*-driven parenting creates an unhealthy level of dependency. That's the problem. Out of fear, some parents never adjust their level of attachment in their kids' lives as the kids get older. They think that by enabling their kids, they are doing them a favor. But it has a reverse effect. Millennials raised by enabling parents are far more likely to rebel, abandon church, and hang with the wrong crowd. They are even less likely to land a sustainable career.

This isn't a blame game. This is getting to the heart of the issue. Because of fear, parents act in a way they expect is best for their kids. It's only years later that parents see the damage their parenting approach has done to an adult child.

Of course, in looking back, many parents would do things differently. That explains the doubts they wrestle with later in life. The *woulda-coulda-shoulda* attitude has plagued this parental generation. We can't tell you how many parents we have counseled who struggle with doubt.

*Did I do enough?*

*Did I do too much?*

*If I only . . .*

*Does my son think I'm a good parent?*

*Does my daughter think I'm a good parent?*

Many Christian parents doubt they were the parents their children needed them to be. What is a workable solution for parents like these going forward?

## Let It Go

Despite the pain, regret, fear, and doubt that may trouble you, rest assured that God is bigger and mightier than your struggles. He is here for you. He has never left your side. He doesn't want you to be trapped by fear. He wants you to turn to Him and trust that He will deliver you from all of your troubles. We read this promise in Psalm 34:4-7: "I sought the LORD, and he answered me and delivered me from all my fears. Those who look to him are radiant, and their faces shall never be ashamed. This poor man cried, and the LORD heard him and saved him out of all his troubles. The angel of the LORD encamps around those who fear him, and delivers them."

*When doubts creep in and you feel you failed as a parent, cry out to the Lord.*

When you feel disappointed in the way you parented, or even ashamed, look to God. When doubts creep in and you feel you failed as a parent, cry out to the Lord. He will heal your pain. Remember, the psalmist says that those who look to God will reflect His glory and will not be ashamed. Every parent needs to hear that. They need to know that they don't have to live a shameful life. What they need to do is let it go and trust that God will restore their family.

## Have Faith

Earlier we talked about *fear*-driven parenting—a place all too familiar to most parents. As we stated above, let God set you free from being led by fear. Stop living in the past. Rather, discover how God can use you in the life of your millennial child right now. Take your focus off *fear*-driven parenting and turn it to *faith*-driven parenting. This is going to be our focus with you: to help you live your life in faith to God.

Let there be no more regrets—only anticipation of the coming blessings. No more doubts—only hope in knowing that God has placed you in your millennial's life for a divine purpose. God has uniquely equipped you to minister to your children. Peter charged the scattered Christians with these words: "As each has received a gift, use it to serve one another, as good stewards of God's varied grace" (1 Peter 4:10). The word *steward* denotes authority and responsibility. As parents, you are God's stewards. You represent Him and have been given the authority and responsibility to serve and to demonstrate His love graciously.

This may be hard for some parents, especially those who struggled with being a strong spiritual leader in their child's life. But we want each of you to know that we have prayed for every parent to be encouraged as he or she goes through this book. We have asked God, in faith, to pour out His Spirit over you. We've asked Him to give you the strength and encouragement needed to be the best steward of His grace to your family.

One of the greatest ways to be a conduit of grace is by living it out for others to see. Paul declared, "Only let your manner of life be worthy of the gospel of Christ" (Philippians 1:27)." The word *manner* literally means "to conduct oneself with proper reference to one's obligations in relationship to others, as part of some community."[3]

Notice that the *manner* or *conduct* of a Christian is in reference to the obligation he or she has to others. In describing Philippians 1:27, *The New Bible Commentary* states, "The gospel has its greatest influence when the lives of Christians commend it, and that gives us our special responsibility. The Greek word translated *conduct yourselves* is the one from which our word 'politics' comes and often conveys the idea of fulfilling one's duty as citizen."[4]

Christians are not only stewards but also citizens. We are called to fulfill our duties as faithful and true citizens of heaven. We don't live for ourselves. We live and serve at the pleasure of Jesus Christ.

Thus, when a Christian parent lives out his or her faith in a way that honors God, it will have a lasting impact on his or her children. There is nothing more powerful.

Yes, the parents of millennials could have done a better job. The data agrees. We all agree. But we are well beyond that now. We trust you have released the discouragement weighing you down and given it over to God.

Before we move to the next chapter, there is one more thing you need to release—and that is your children.

## Release Your Children

Could you imagine giving up your child? It is hard to imagine. Yet that's exactly what two couples—Elkanah and Hannah and Amram and Jochebed—had to do.

In Exodus 2:2, we read, "The woman [Jochebed] conceived and bore a son; and when she saw that he was a fine child, she hid him three months [to protect him from the Egyptians]" (brackets added). Jochebed and her family were under oppressive rule. Fearing the rapidly growing population of Hebrews, Pharaoh gave the order for the Egyptians to kill all newly born Hebrew boys. But when Moses' parents could no longer hide him, his sister put him in a basket—praying someone would care for him (Exodus 2:3-4). What incredible faith Amram and Jochebed had. The writer of Hebrews puts it this way: "By faith Moses' parents hid him for three months after he was born, because they saw he was no ordinary child, and they were not afraid of the king's edict" (11:23, NIV).

*Rather than be paralyzed by fear, they released their son to God.*

Did you catch that? Moses' parents saw how special their baby boy was, and they did not fear the Pharaoh's edict. Rather than be paralyzed by fear, they released their son to God. And the rest is history.

Then there is Hannah, a woman, according to 1 Samuel 1, who was unable to have children. This was a disgraceful position in those days. Infertile women were considered a curse—lawbreakers. It was their legal obligation to produce an offspring for their husbands. Yet Hannah remained barren. She continued to pray for God to grant her and her husband a son, a child they could hold and love one day.

In 1 Samuel 1:10-11, we read, "She [Hannah] was deeply distressed and prayed to the LORD and wept bitterly. And she vowed a vow and said, 'O LORD of hosts, if you will indeed look on the affliction of your servant and remember me and not forget your servant, but will give to your servant a son, then I will give him to the LORD all the days of his life, and no razor shall touch his head.'"

Finally, after much prayer and vexation, the Lord answered Hannah's prayer.

Why did God answer Hannah's prayer? Because Hannah cared more about serving God than parenting a child. Hannah prayed for a son, but she also promised to give her son right back to God. Before Samuel was conceived in Hannah's womb, she had already released him back to God. That's what you call faith!

Now your story may not be that dramatic. But the lesson is the same. As Amram and Jochebed did with Moses—so must you do with your children. As Hannah prayed, "I will give him to the Lord," so must you pray, "Lord, I give my children to you. I release them back to you."

Children are a gift. But they are also on loan. You don't own your children. They may have your DNA. But they are made in the image of God. You would lay your life down for your kids. But Jesus laid His life down and rose again so that your kids may have eternal life.

Before you go any further, give each of your children completely and totally over to God. You will be glad you did.

# Chapter 2

# WHY MILLENNIALS ARE LEAVING THE FAITH

DOES THE FOLLOWING email message break your heart? It certainly does ours.

> I have a 22-year-old son who left the faith in college. Ironically, so many hurts that were inflicted by believers, and the hypocrisy my son saw among his peers, drove him away. He was admired in high school for his walk with Christ. He was my only child of five who went to a secular college. Please pray for my son. I believe Jesus will bring him back to the fold. God is working on me to trust Him. It is very terrifying as a parent in regard to his soul.

This sad message came from a mom whose son left the faith for reasons he clearly explained to her. Her concern and despair echo the emotions of many parents who may or may not understand what caused their own children to abandon faith.

As we examine the question "Why?" we'll see that the causes are as diverse as millennials themselves. It may be confusing to our children as well, as many fail to understand the reasons behind their own disconnection from faith roots.

For instance, I (Jason) spoke at a Cru (Campus Crusade for Christ) event at a campus in Florida, where several students stayed behind to ask questions. One guy was very argumentative. Event leaders tried to answer his questions, but no matter what they said, the student continued to argue his point of view.

After I heard him say, "That's not my truth; that's your truth," I asked if he was ready to talk with me personally. He agreed, along with his girlfriend. I could tell she was upset. It was clear they were wrestling with big issues. Their key question was, "If God exists, and He knew we would suffer, then why did He create us?"

Before taking a stab at answering this deep and philosophical question, I asked them if they were raised in Christian homes. They both said yes. I then asked if both sets of parents were still married. The guy said yes, but told me his parents argued a lot. The girl said her parents divorced when she was in middle school.

After getting some background, I asked this pointed question: "Do you believe truth exists?"

The guy answered, "I believe truth is expressed individually."

I responded, "Is what you just said true?"

He danced around the question a bit, and then said that it was true for him.

To make sure I understood what he believed, I asked him one more time, "So, you are saying that what you believe is only true for you, not for anyone else. Is that true?"

He looked away for a moment, then said, "Yes." Eventually he saw his contradiction. Truth can't be relative, but it is absolute. It applies to all people, at all times, and in all places.

After a few minutes, we shifted to their original question about pain and suffering. As we talked, the couple expressed a lot of bitterness, especially the girl. I tried hard not to make them feel uncomfortable, but I felt the Holy Spirit pressing me to dig more deeply into their upbringing.

Both of them came from legalistic backgrounds. The girl's dad lectured the family about the Bible, yet he left her mother for another woman. The guy's family went to church, but beyond that, he never saw his parents reading the Bible or praying as a family.

*If God is so loving, why didn't their parents show that same love to each other?*

I could see now why they questioned God, His nature, and His *unconditional* love. If what their parents believed was true, why didn't they live it? If God is so loving, why didn't their parents show that same love to each other?

That was the main problem. It wasn't really whether God

exists or whether the Bible can be trusted. The real issue with these two young college students involved their unresolved issues with their parents. It's understandable that, as college students exposed to different worldviews, they had moved away from childhood faith. It doesn't make it right, but it certainly reveals why many millennials like them feel as they do and believe what they believe.

Beneath the questions, many young people carry an insane amount of confusion, hurt, and rejection. They might also have bits and pieces of the truth, but because they were never taught and discipled in the Christian faith, they now lack a biblical worldview.

An interview with David Kinnaman, president of the Barna Group, adds to our understanding of the breadth of the issue. I (Jason) asked him, "According to your research, what are some key reasons why millennials are less Christian today than in their parents' and grandparents' generations?"

Kinnaman outlined three major differences in the generations:

At the Barna Group, our research shows correlations, and cannot definitively say what the reasons are for loss of faith among millions of millennials. We can, however, listen in to their stories, their experiences and their perceptions and we can look at larger social changes that are taking place. In the book *You Lost Me*, Gabe Lyons and I observe that there are three things that are different today than for previous generations: 1) greater levels of access to ideas and worldviews, particularly through the Internet; 2) intensified degree of alienation from institutions and relationships; and 3) more skepticism of authority, whether that is from the government, church or the Bible. These three conditions are creating the soil in which a more skeptical, post-Christian mind-set is taking root.

Let's explore together major causes for faith abandonment common among millennial Christians.

## Seven Key Reasons

I (Jason) grappled with this issue along with Dr. Norman Geisler in a book we wrote together: *The Bible's Answers to 100 of Life's Biggest Questions.* The answer to Question 95—"Why Are So Many Young People Abandoning the Faith?"—brought to light the following reasons:

1. Many millennials (18- to 29-year-olds) who claim to be Christians never had a true conversion to begin with. The pat Sunday school prayers that churches and revivals have people recite don't guarantee salvation. Many young people never come to a point where they truly believe in Jesus Christ (Acts 16:31), repent from their sins, and give their lives to God (Acts 3:19; 8:22).

2. The simple fact is that a large majority of Christian parents have done a poor job living out their faith and raising their children in the Bible (Ephesians 6:4). Many millennials have been raised to be legalistic rather than to live a biblical life. There's been a greater emphasis on rewarding good behavior than on being obedient to God's Word. As a result, many young people rebel and fail to see the discipline of God's grace in their lives.

3. Doubts about the Bible and common objections about Christianity often get the best of millennials. You would think that after being raised in Christian homes and attending church for years, most millennials would have a strong faith in the Bible. But the fact is that they don't. When asked about this, young people say they never really felt they could express their doubts and concerns regarding Christianity at home or in the church. This caused a level of intellectual skepticism to sprout up and choke any roots of faith that may have been left.

4. Millennials fail to see the connection faith has to culture. Their lack of involvement in the church damages their ability to connect faith to day-to-day life. When millennials grow up, they have no idea the role faith should play in their careers, personal interests, or future lives.

5. Hypocrisy and compromise in the church play a significant role in many millennials abandoning

the faith. They see the church as more concerned about money and membership than about teaching the Bible.

6. The majority of millennials are biblically illiterate. Most of them have neglected reading and applying the Bible. So, of course, when a competing belief or religion comes their way, millennials are unable to defend the Christian faith. One way Satan has been able to do this is through the false teaching of naturalism—an ideology that teaches there is no God, absolute truth, meaning, or afterlife.

7. Millennials have never actually been taught about the life, work, death, and resurrection of Jesus Christ. The focus has been more on the celebrity pastor than on the Savior, Jesus Christ. More time and resources have been devoted to launching satellite campuses than to training up the next generation in the Word of God. The result: millennials never encounter Jesus.[1]

These reasons that millennials leave the faith stand out among additional possibilities. As we explore them in depth, you may better understand your own child's reasoning and, we hope, engage him or her in meaningful conversation.

Of course, a related question involves why young people are leaving the church itself. We will cover that issue more specifically in chapter 4.

## Shallow Faith Lived Out in Name Only

Millennials frequently tell us they got the short end of the stick when it came to their faith development. According to their recollections, the Bible was little more than an Instagram post in their lives. Their parents' faith seemed similar to pledging allegiance to a club. They paid their dues, attended a few meetings throughout the year, and on occasion, participated in some lavish party. It wasn't even a club they wanted to join, as one father said. His three older kids were repelled from church by the actions of arrogant and self-righteous members.

These young people clearly observed that the faith they grew up in was a cultural activity instead of a truly spiritual one.

I (Jason) saw this in practice when I moved my family from Arizona to North Carolina. The ministry I came from had been down-to-earth, and most of the families came from difficult backgrounds. We heard incredible salvation stories every week. If you attended church there, it was because you were a follower of Christ. Period.

*Most of these people claiming to be Christians were Christian in name only.*

When I moved to the Bible Belt, I was in for a surprise. Everybody claimed they were Christians. I told my wife I never knew there were so many Christians living in one city. It was pretty awesome. Until I realized that most of these people *claiming* to be Christians were Christian in name only. Though many people had religious and denominational affiliations, they had very few conversion stories.

This eye-opening experience stems from 40-plus years of cultural Christianity. We believe in God. We believe in right and wrong. We don't like feeling guilty. We even put Jesus on the top of our list of people to emulate. Yet the gospel of Jesus Christ is not evident. The gospel has been neglected, and it is no longer defended as it ought to be.

The fact of cultural Christianity speaks directly to the confusion and resentment millennials are facing. To reach them in the face of this challenge requires us to first reach the parents. We need to speak to your heart—so you can become the mom or dad the Lord has called you to be in the life of your adult child or children.

## The Role of Parents as Faith Influencers

There is no denying that culture and church play a major role in the developmental life of any person. But the role parents play in their children's lives far outweighs any other influence. What parents *believe* and how they live out their *beliefs* (positively or negatively) has a huge impact on their children.

In the groundbreaking book *Lost in Translation: The Dark Side of Emerging Adulthood*, sociological expert and director of the Center for the Study of Religion and Society, Dr. Christian Smith, offers a simple yet often forgotten piece of advice:

Most of the problems in the lives of youth have
their origins in the larger adult world into which the
youth are being socialized. It might be the problems

of the adults in their immediate lives—their parents, relatives, teachers, family friends, and so on. Or it might be the priorities, values, practices, and institutions of the larger adult world they inhabit—schools, mass media, shopping malls, advertising, and the like. But one way or another, adults and the adult world are almost always complicit in the troubles, suffering, and misguided living of youth, if not the direct source of them. The more adults can recognize and admit that fact—the sooner we will be able to address some of young people's problems more constructively.[2]

If one-on-one care and modeling from adults (such as teachers, coaches, and pastors) are extremely important for young people, how much more so when it comes to parenting?

*Parents are the most influential and most powerful force in a child's life.*

You see, parents are the key. Parents are the most influential and most powerful force in a child's life. Nothing can compare to the love a mother has for her children. Nothing comes close to the security and wisdom a father provides for his children. So as we examine this mass exodus from faith and church, let's not forget that mom and dad are a key factor.

A few years ago, we hosted a "Truth for a New Generation" conference in Charlotte, North Carolina. I (Jason) had the opportunity to interview Sean McDowell, a dear friend to both of us. We spoke about the challenges of ministering to millennials. Here's our dialogue:

*Jason:* Sean, one of the trends we are seeing is that of young people leaving the church. Why do you think that is?

*Sean:* It's important to make the distinction between leaving the *faith* and leaving the *church*. There are many studies from Barna Group and Fuller Institute that show over half of millennials, when entering college, leave the church. Now there certainly are those millennials who leave the faith, but it's a smaller percentage. Studies are showing that very few are coming back. They did so in the past, but not so much today, which is a big concern. There are a lot of reasons for this. It can be for moral reasons—the kid doesn't believe it's right. It can be volitional reasons—the kid doesn't want to live it. It can be relational, spiritual, or intellectual. When it gets right down to it, David Kinnaman, in his book *You Lost Me*, hit it exactly. He said the bottom line is we failed to help young people see that Christianity is a comprehensive way of living all of life. In other words, millennials see no connection to what you believe spiritually and how you actually live. They've seen how spiritual things help on Sunday morning and Wednesday night, but don't see how it translates into their everyday lives, like how they compete on the field, or perform in school, or behave in their relationships. Faith hasn't been as impactful as mom and dad hoped, so when their child goes off to the university, their faith comes under attack. They are faced with different kinds of worldviews and moral challenges, and it's extremely tough, especially if they have an undeveloped faith. So, of course, many of these young people are going to disengage.

*Jason:* So what can parents do?

*Sean:* The most important thing parents should do is model Christianity to their kids—to engage them with a biblical worldview.

*Jason:* The biggest influencers in a child's life are mom and dad, even when that child gets older. So how can mom and dad get more involved, as you say, modeling Christianity to their kids who are in or out of college?

*Sean:* Significant spiritual conversation is so important, especially if they are still in college. They need that. Young people crave conversation with significant others in their life. They don't want lectures, but actual conversations. This is biblical. We see that daily interactions about spiritual matters are important (as in Deuteronomy 6). It's something God commanded parents to do with their children. So I would tell parents to find ways to just talk with their children in a fun and friendly way. There have to be a lot of questions. Not questioning but questions that keep the conversation going, and help parents see the reasoning behind their child's decision making. Again, you can't expect to have these kinds of conversations if you aren't living it. I've seen parents preach one thing and live another. You better believe those kids saw the hypocrisy from their mom and dad.

Sean hit on some very important points, including one of the most devastating reasons young people leave the Christian faith: Some parents have failed to help their children see Christianity in a holistic, true, and meaningful way.

Prior to the mass exodus of millennials from the church, there was a mass exodus of fathers leaving their families. Before millennials stopped attending church, their fathers had already stopped making church a priority. Before the doubts took hold of millennials, fear and doubt were already embedded in their parents' lives.

## A Disconnected Family

There are way too many choices in America. Just go to the nearest grocery store and pick from the endless variety of cereals, ketchups, shampoos, sodas, and chips (with dip, of course).

The same goes for today's kids. There are endless school choices, limitless programs for musicians, and dozens of athletic programs to choose from. The fast pace of life grows uncontrollably as parents rush their kids from school to practice and back again. Family time becomes a series of drop-offs and pick-ups. With deadlines at work, laundry piling up, and homework to be finished, the obligations of life can drive families apart. Family dinners fizzle out. Relaxation and quality time is no longer a priority, and those deep conversations about things that matter turn into routine arguments.

*Parents begin to lose sight of their roles in their kids' lives.*

In the hustle and bustle of kids' activities, parents begin to lose sight of their roles in their kids' lives. With attention focused on enrolling kids in the *top programs*, they lose sight of being the *top mom or dad* their kids need them to be. Parents may intend well, but the results they hope for often don't materialize. Looking back, many parents wish they hadn't kept their kids in so many extra activities year round.

With so many choices and instant access to information and entertainment, millennials in the United States have become the most educated and entitled generation ever. Since they were born, millennials have been showered with praises. They were raised believing there are no winners or losers, just participants who get trophies for showing up.

Millennials were also raised with the idea that their education, dreams, and talents are as important as faith. Think about it. If your child grew up investing time, energy, and focus in sports, school, music, dance, gaming, or anything else that overshadowed developing his or her faith—then essentially that activity was more important than spiritual growth.

This truth came to light when I (Jason) was trying to get several of my older students to go to summer camp. The majority of the parents said, "I really hope they can go to camp, but it's up to their schedule." When I talked to the students, they would tell me, "If sports camp isn't going on, then I will go."

These types of responses were acceptable to most families who attended my church. At some point, parents made a conscious decision to allow something other than church be the driving force for their children's lives. By the time that son or daughter entered the sixth grade, sports became the dominant driver in that child's life.

*How have those priorities in your child's earlier years played out in his or her life today?*

Years later, how have those priorities in your child's earlier years played out in his or her life today? The Pew Research Center conducted a study examining the most important things in the lives of millennials. Here's what they found:

- 52 percent want to be a good parent
- 30 percent want to have a successful marriage
- 21 percent want to help others in need
- 20 percent want to own a home
- 15 percent want to live a very religious life
- 15 percent want to have a high-paying career
- 9 percent want to have lots of free time
- 1 percent want to become famous[3]

It's pretty cool that the most important thing for over half of millennials surveyed was to be a good parent. The tragedy, however, is that marriage (30 percent) and faith (15 percent) were not as important. This reveals a major disconnect. We discover that millennials want to have children, but they lack the drive to support a faith and marriage to go with a family.

Why? Because more than half of millennials come from divorced or single families. If they do come from homes where their parents are still married, many express that they don't admire their parents' marriages.

When we examine the millions of millennials either leaving the faith or the church, we see that brokenness and disconnection are the two primary contributors. This is where the transfer of faith has broken down.

## Bibles Galore, but Reading It Is No More

*Millennials and the Bible* was a study from Barna Group conducted in partnership with the American Bible Society and InterVarsity Christian Fellowship. In this study, the group found some interesting dynamics when it comes to millennials' perception of and engagement with the Bible:

- "Most millennials believe the Bible to be the actual (21 percent) or inspired (44 percent) word of God."
- "The gap is widening between millennials who are engaged with the Bible (10 percent) and those who are considered Bible skeptics (25 percent)."

- "Approximately one-third of millennials have positive feelings when they see someone reading the Bible in public."
- "Non-Christian millennials believe the Bible teaches forgiveness (70 percent), patience (62 percent), generosity (64 percent) and social justice (41 percent)."[4]

If this generation is going to return to God, they need to open the pages of God's Word once again. Pray with us that this will change.

## A Culture of Stress

One thing that millennials stress about is the approval of others—particularly mom and dad. That may be hard to believe, but the truth is, millennials tell us all the time about how worried they get if mom or dad don't approve. Parental approval weighs heavily on them. Which is great. It shows they still care and want and need their parents' approval.

In 2015, the American Psychological Association (APA) dubbed millennials the most stressed-out generation in America. Can you believe that? An APA study called *Stress in America* compiled several key findings about millennials:

- Millennials and Gen-Xers report the highest levels of stress.
- Millennials are the most likely of all generations to say their stress has increased in the past year.

- Millennials are more likely than any other generation to say they have felt a sense of loneliness/isolation due to stress in the past month.
- More than four-fifths of millennials (82 percent) say they have experienced at least one symptom of stress in the past month.
- Millennials are more likely than other generations to say that stress has a very strong or strong impact on their physical and mental health.
- More than half of millennials say they have lain awake at night in the past month due to stress.[5]

So what are millennials turning to in order to cope with stress? Xanax. Sure, many millennials will try listening to calm music, hanging with friends, perhaps texting mom or dad for guidance, or even praying to God. But more and more of them are slipping into unsafe patterns that will only do more harm than good. And we all know that abusing prescription drugs is not the answer.

## Underdeveloped Brain

Does your child seem to be experiencing delayed adolescence? Ever wonder why he or she never really matured out of the teen years? Let's look into the contributing factors, starting with a clear definition of adolescence.

Dr. Chap Clark, in his well-researched book *Hurt 2.0*, states, "Adolescence, then, is a psychosocial, independent search for a unique identity or separateness, with the end goals being a certain knowledge of who one is in relation to others, a willingness to take responsibility for who one is becoming, and a realized commitment to live with others in community."[6]

John Santrock, a developmental psychologist, defines adolescence as "the period of life between childhood and adulthood. . . . [The process] lasts from roughly 10–13 years of age and ends at 18–22 years of age. [However,] defining when adolescence ends is not an easy task. It has been said that adolescence begins in biology and ends in culture."[7]

*This generation has been stuck in adolescence a lot longer than any previous generation.*

Your child may have graduated from college, gotten a job, paid income taxes, and even gotten married, but that doesn't mean he or she has graduated from adolescence. You see, this generation has been stuck in adolescence a lot longer than any previous generation. This isn't good. (We can hear all the "amens"!)

Brain development is a key factor contributing to delayed adolescence. In his funny but provocative book *Yes, Your Teen Is Crazy!*, Dr. Michael Bradley records the two groundbreaking discoveries of Dr. Jay Giedd (National Institute of Mental Health) and McGill University in Canada. He writes:

They saw that throughout the teen years and into the twenties, substantial growth occurs in the brain structure called the corpus callosum. The corpus callosum is a set of nerves that connects all the parts of the brain that must work together to function efficiently, as in making good decisions. This set of "wires" is critical to things like intelligence, consciousness, and self-awareness. . . . With amazement they also found that the prefrontal cortex of the brain goes through a wild growth that coincides with the onset of adolescence. In fact, they found that this part of the brain does the bulk of its maturation between the ages of 12 and 20. The prefrontal cortex is where the most sophisticated of our abilities reside. Emotional control, impulse restraint, and rational decision making, are all gifts to us from our prefrontal cortex, gifts your kid hasn't yet received.[8]

It's important to understand the underdeveloped brain because it affects the identity formation of every young person. If you have a twentysomething right now, your son or daughter is still figuring out who he or she is, what he or she likes, and what he or she should do. Choices and decisions are affected in a big way by the maturity of your child's brain.

How many stupid things has your son or daughter done in his or her lifetime? Out of those times, how often did you ask, "What were you thinking?" In most cases, when your son or daughter did something very irresponsible—he or she simply wasn't thinking. Now an underdeveloped brain doesn't excuse poor behavior or lessen certain consequences. Your millennial is old enough to know right from wrong and might even pray and seek wisdom from God (see James 1:5). But some millennials are still growing. With brains that are still maturing, these kids need mom and dad to help them make the right decisions.

According to psychologist Laurence Steinberg of Temple University, by the late twenties, "There's better communication between parts of the brain that process emotions and social information—like what people think of you—and the parts that are important for planning ahead and balancing risk and reward."[9]

In certain areas of life millennials are not progressing as quickly as previous generations did. This is causing many parents to be concerned, and has resulted in a rise of depression among millennials. So, instead of judging your child and bringing out the lectern to preach fire and brimstone, remember that he or she can't think as you think.

It may be that your child really could use your help. He needs you, mom and dad. She needs you to be patient with her. Give your adult child the benefit of the doubt.

## Underdeveloped Faith

This generation has a yearning to *believe* in a religion that is true. The problem is, a growing number of millennials don't know which religion that is.

Stop and think about that for a moment. After all the years in church, with millions upon millions of dollars spent on private Christian education, camps, retreats, and so on—nearly 20 percent of millennials under age 30 are no longer affiliated with the religion they were brought up to believe.

Moreover, these same young adults who left the religion of their upbringing didn't trade it in for another religion. The majority of millennials, raised in a Christian home, became dissatisfied with Christianity because of their doubts, their skepticism, and the hypocrisy they witnessed in the church. They simply abandoned their faith.

In a classic book about the stages of a child's faith, Dr. James Fowler does a really good job charting the unique stages of developmental faith in the life of an individual.[10]

**STAGES OF DEVELOPMENTAL FAITH**
**FIG. 1**

| | |
|---|---|
| Stage One (Child): *Intuitive-Projective Faith* | A simple faith that totally buys into parents' faith and those nurturing influences closest to them. |
| Stage Two (Middle/Late Childhood): *Mythical-Literal Faith* | A church faith that broadens the scope of influence and grows from imaginative to more linear curiosity. |
| Stage Three (Mid-Adolescence): *Synthetic-Conventional Faith* | An exploratory faith that synthesizes values and information and grapples to find answers. |

| Stage Four (Late-Adolescence/Early Adulthood): *Individuative-Reflective Faith* | An individual faith that comprises ownership, responsibility, and consequences. |
|---|---|
| Stage Five (Middle Adulthood): *Conjunctive Faith* | A tested faith that has taken shape and is building to live out a consistent worldview of ideas and measured performance. |
| Stage Six (Late Adulthood): *Universalizing Faith* | A universal faith that is lived out convincingly and contagiously to all those they interact with. |

Dr. Fowler's chart offers us great insight into faith development for most people. However, our ministry with millennials has shown us that it doesn't apply to this group. We have revised Dr. Fowler's chart and modified it to fit the faith stages (or lack thereof) for millennials. See Figure 2 below.[11]

**STAGES OF NON-DEVELOPMENTAL FAITH OF MILLENNIALS**
**FIG. 2**

| Stage One (Child): *Emerging Faith* | A simple faith that remained lacking because the parents' faith was inconsistent. |
|---|---|
| Stage Two (Middle/Late Childhood): *Learning Faith* | A church faith that should have broadened the scope of influence but wasn't as much of a priority as was sports, work, relationships, trips, etc. |

| | |
|---|---|
| Stage Three (Mid-Adolescence): *Questioning Faith* | A probing faith that didn't get the answers and information it was seeking out. |
| Stage Four (Late-Adolescence/Early Adulthood): *Doubting Faith* | An uncertain faith that lacks ownership, responsibility, and consequences. |
| Stage Five (Middle Adulthood): *Rejecting Faith* | An untested faith that will shape their lives, and bring about a worldview that will run contrary to the Bible. *(Older millennials are about to enter this stage).* |
| Stage Six (Late Adulthood): *Longing Faith* | A disavowed faith that will be lived out with resentment and will impact the coming generations. *(Hopefully most millennials will never arrive here when they get older).* |

Like many hurting parents in the church, you may have experienced these rough and emotional stages with your millennial child. Of course, this is a generalization and may not be true of every millennial. But it certainly is true for millions of them.

## Underdeveloped Values

Mom and dad, we have some blunt questions for you:

- Did you ever talk to your son or daughter about sex when he or she was younger?
- Did you ever have to deal with porn in your home?
- Do you know if your millennial child has an addiction?

We make no apologies for these questions. Too many millennials today are involved with porn, sexting, or hook-ups and other premarital sex, and the sad truth is, not many parents ever had those intimate talks with their kids.

I (Jason) remember meeting with several parents over lunch. The meeting was designed to help the church come alongside and equip them to talk with their children about dating, marriage, and sex. The church was offering a conference for parents and their teenage or college-age kids. Parents who were thinking about registering needed to attend a mandatory meeting. This lunch was to help them determine whether they wanted their teens involved.

Afterward, a father, one I had known for years, came up to me. He was concerned that the topic of sex had no place in the church. He said it was a private matter and that we needed to stick to the Bible.

I asked my friend one simple question: "Do you want your daughter to learn about sex from discussions with you and your wife? Or do you want her to learn about it by engaging in the culture?" I wanted this father to understand that the church was gathering parents together and talking about sex in the context of the Bible and marriage. We were equipping parents, not stripping them of their responsibility to teach their children about the purity and beauty of sex in marriage.

This generation, which you helped to raise, is under heavy sexual bondage.

*This generation, which you helped to raise, is under heavy sexual bondage.*

Everybody knows this, yet not many are willing to dive right in and help. It's awkward. It's embarrassing. And it's a very difficult conversation to have with your children. However, if we want millennials (including your son or daughter) to avoid the path of sexual addiction, we must face the facts and get involved.

One of the things that we observe because of the *porn craze* among millennials is that young women feel they don't measure up. They feel cheap and alone. One girl in her twenties came up after a Stand Strong Tour and shared how she'd been dragged into the human sex trade. She said it all started because she was looking for love. A man she was dating got her hooked into it. Thankfully, she was delivered out of sex trafficking—yet she still struggles with feeling empty and unloved.

On the other hand, guys are not looking for a committed relationship. Intimacy is not something they typically want. Instead, they pursue fantasy and virtual sex. With one tap of a button they can instantly get whatever suits their fancy right on their device. They don't have to wine and dine girls. There are no arguments and long good-byes. Just instant sexual entertainment.

Read how Naomi Wolf, in her piece *The Porn Myth*, recalls Andrea Dworkin's (a 1980s anti-porn activist) warnings about polarized porn in America. She also paints a graphic picture of the effects porn is having on men.

As she [Andrea Dworkin] foretold, pornography
did breach the dike that separated a marginal,

adult, private pursuit from the mainstream public arena. The whole world, post-Internet, did become pornographized. Young men and women are indeed being taught what sex is, how it looks, what its etiquette and expectations are, by pornographic training—and this is having a huge effect on how they interact.

But the effect is not making men into raving beasts. On the contrary: The onslaught of porn is responsible for deadening male libido in relation to real women, and leading men to see fewer and fewer women as "porn-worthy." Far from having to fend off porn-crazed young men, young women are worrying that as mere flesh and blood, they can scarcely get, let alone hold, their attention.[12]

The sacredness and purity of sex within marriage is seemingly lost in the culture embraced by today's millennials. Deep down, that's what they truly want, but they don't know how to achieve it. So many young people aren't getting married because they feel they ruined their chances by sleeping around. One college student said, "I feel like used goods. Who would want to marry me?"

After leading premarital sessions with twentysomethings, we estimate at least three out of four young couples are having sex outside of marriage. We're talking about professed Christians having sex before they are married! It's as if no one

*God calls each and every one of us to be holy, as He is holy.*

cares anymore. Everyone is doing it, so why does it matter?

It does matter. God calls each and every one of us to be holy, as He is holy. First Thessalonians 4:3 reads, "For this is the will of God, your sanctification: that you abstain from sexual immorality." Hebrews 13:4 states, "Let marriage be held in honor among all, and let the marriage bed be undefiled, for God will judge the sexually immoral and adulterous."

Yet cybersex and hook-ups are destroying the moral conscience of the millennial generation. Today the door is open to a variety of sexually liberated lifestyles, including homosexuality, bisexuality, and polyamorous relationships.

We realize you can't just call your son or daughter and point-blank ask your child to share openly about his or her sex life.

If you do sense that your son or daughter is having premarital sex or is addicted to porn, gently remind him or her that you are always there to talk with. Look for fun and nonthreatening ways to discuss deeper issues about God, sex, relationships, stress, and the pressures of life. Help your child work through his or her issues by sharing that you have struggles and that you were once twenty-something yourself. Don't just tell him what he should do, but tell him your story, your temptations, and how Jesus delivered you out of whatever mess you were in. Always remind your children that they are loved and prayed over constantly.

## Understanding "Why" Can Lead Us to Hope

In his eye-opening bestseller *Already Gone,* Ken Ham dealt with the tragedy of two-thirds of young people leaving the church. In that book he offered some remedies to stop the mass exodus. In his last book in the series, *Ready to Return,* Ken presents some troubling statistics from America's Research Group of regular church attenders in the twentysomething category.

- 65 percent believe that if you are a good person you will go to heaven.
- 50 percent do not believe in a young earth.
- 43 percent do not consider themselves born again.
- 30 percent believe people don't need to go to church.
- 23 percent believe God used evolution to change one kind of animal to another kind.
- 19 percent believe humans evolved from ape-like ancestors.
- 40 percent support gay "marriage," and 10 percent aren't sure (in other words, 50 percent would not stand against gay "marriage").[13]

These statistics are troubling. If anything, they reveal that we have a lot of work to do. But rather than travel down a path of negativity, we would rather point out a few positives. By doing so, we can better address these troubling numbers with the right solutions.

For example, though young people attending the church

have a very weak view of Christian beliefs, they do believe in God. As a matter of fact, over 80 percent of young people believe in God, while about 10 percent either believe in a vague "higher power" or else consider themselves agnostic or atheist.[14]

Reporting on the faith millennials have in God, the Pew Research Center had this to say: "Though belief in God is lower among young adults than among older adults, millennials say they believe in God with absolute certainty at rates similar to those seen among Gen-Xers a decade ago. This suggests that some of the religious differences between younger and older Americans today are not entirely generational but result in part from people's tendency to place greater emphasis on religion as they age."[15]

*"I'd love to help my adult child develop her faith, but she's too hostile."*

Now as a parent, you may think, "I'd love to help my adult child develop her faith, but she's too hostile." No doubt that may feel true for some, but before you die on that claim, let's look into whether that is actually true.

In a comprehensive survey about non-favorability to religious groups, Dr. Bradley Wright, a sociologist at the University of Connecticut, took the findings from Pew Religion and Public Life (2007), divided the non-Christian respondents from the Christian respondents, and placed them into three age groups: 18–29, 30–49, and 50 or older. In his own findings, Dr. Wright found that it's actually the 50-and-up category of evangelical Christians who have an overall unfavorable opinion about other religions.

Of course, this survey was not an attempt for evangelicals to agree with the doctrinal positions of Jews, Mormons, Muslims, etc. The purpose was to see how the different ages *felt* toward other religious views. What Dr. Wright discovered was that young people are actually more open and less judgmental when it comes to religious conversation than their parents and definitely their grandparents.

This is great news. For far too long, the older generation has carried this false belief that the younger generation doesn't want to have religious conversations with them. We hear excuses from parents all the time: "I really want to bring up the conversation about God, but my son or daughter doesn't want to hear it."

Really? Are you sure? Approach, attitude and respect are everything. That's nothing new. We all have opinions, and we all have the right to express them. The problem occurs when someone disrespects another person's opinion or insults his or her religious views. Those are fighting words.

Your millennial may be rejecting Christianity and may seem to favor other religious views (kind of like embracing an "all religions are true, except for Christianity" point of view). Rather than try and prove him or her wrong, remember this: that kind of thinking *proves* that your son or daughter has an underdeveloped faith. So be hopeful that the seed of faith still has time to grow. Meanwhile, focus on getting a better understanding of why your son or daughter has walked away from the faith.

# Chapter 3

# WHAT LIES BEHIND ABANDONED FAITH?

THE STATISTICS YOU READ in chapter 2 underline this unfortunate truth: millennials are leaving the church, abandoning Christian values, and increasingly living apart from any particular religious tradition. We've not only heard these views; we've also witnessed them firsthand over the past two decades of serving teenagers and young adults across America. The shift is real, growing, and disturbing in many ways.

As a parent, you are likely far less concerned with the results of the latest survey than you are with the outcome for your own child. We want to provide you a breadth of information and insight so you can apply what you learn to your own family situation. And as we dig deeper into the challenging issues surrounding abandoned faith, remember that God can work in and through your millennial child in powerful ways. Whether your concerns are focused on your child's salvation, relationships, vocation, or responsibilities, be encouraged that God's truth provides answers for your child and for your role in the process. You are not alone in this journey.

While researching and writing this book, I (Alex) had the opportunity to interview three experts who are on the front lines in the battle to win millennials for the kingdom of God. In our time together, we addressed some of the most significant changes taking place in the culture and our churches. We explored the impact of these changes on the way parents, church leaders, teachers, coaches, and youth workers can best relate to those young people who make up the millennial generation.

As you tap into our dialogues, consider how these first-hand observations affect your view of your child and the changing world that has shaped him or her.

## The Generational Shift

Dr. Ed Stetzer is the executive director of the Billy Graham Center for Evangelism and the bestselling author of numerous books that chronicle the spiritual shifts taking place in our culture.

In our discussion, Dr. Stetzer addressed the generational shift that many Christian parents and churches have failed to recognize and react to. He stated, "If the 1950s come back, a lot of churches are ready to go!" Many churches are doing things just as they were done 50 years ago (or more). The style of worship and the ways we try to share the message haven't changed. Even the décor of our church buildings have remained frozen in time. But what has dramatically transformed is the culture all around the church.

**Many millennials see the church as an irrelevant relic of the past.**

Many millennials see the church as an irrelevant relic of the past. Meanwhile, too many Christians have forgotten that the goal of the church is to help people follow Christ rather than show up for an hour on Sunday.

Dr. Stetzer notes that disengagement and apathy contribute to abandoned faith, but other factors are also at work. Christians of all generations are to reach out with the gospel in the surrounding neighborhoods where their churches are located. Yet today, many church members live far from those neighborhoods. The churches don't really impact their surroundings because, other than maintaining a building, the people who go there don't connect with the people outside its four walls.

Further, Stetzer notes that many churches don't pray for or reach out to the community they are called to minister to. At least one of these communities surrounds the area where every church property sits. The downside of our commuting culture is that it leads us to believe the church we attend on Sunday has no connection with the people we seek to impact the rest of the week.

## The Spiritual Shift

Important spiritual shifts are taking place among today's twentysomethings. Stetzer recognizes that millennials think and feel differently. Their behaviors, buying habits, and brand loyalty (or lack of it) are far less predictable than those of previous generations.

Stetzer's research and experiences have led him to urge us to ask the right questions. For example, we can debate which style of music or building will best connect with millennials, but the greater challenge is to understand how to better *connect with one another*. Relationships have always been at the heart of the gospel and how we share the Good News of Jesus.

In many cases, however, our churches do not naturally facilitate relationships. We tend to deliver products—religious goods and services—rather than the authentic relationships the rising generation desires and needs. Millennials couldn't care less about how "cool" or "relevant" the band or student ministry is. They care more about whether a congregation helps the poor and welcomes first-time visitors. Authentic relationships are central to effective ministry.

Stetzer further notes that their surveys have shown that 89 percent of the unchurched are willing to have a conversation with a friend about Christianity. Regardless of their spiritual status, millennials remain spiritually hungry.

I've often realized this with audiences I (Alex) speak with across the country. Whenever question-and-answer sessions begin and the microphone is open, spiritual hunger is unleashed in the form of genuine, probing questions. Some of these sessions have lasted more than an hour. In an audience of 300 teenagers or young adults, usually 25 to 50 hands are raised after each question. After our official question-and-answer time ends, Jason and I will stand in the lobby late into the night, praying and talking individually with young people. They deeply desire to understand spiritual issues through the context of authentic relationships.

In spite of this spiritual hunger, Stetzer points out that many churches and individual believers talk themselves out of even trying to reach this generation. Negative statistics or stories may convince us that the mission is impossible. The truth is that we are right—unless we build strong relationships with those we seek to impact.

*Though difficult, our calling is to make disciples from among all people and all ages.*

Though difficult, our calling is to make disciples from among all people and all ages. How are we intentionally building cross-generational relationships? It should encourage us to know that many young adults desire relationships with mentors—older people who are perceived as wise and experienced. Churches have an extraordinary opportunity to foster this kind of mentorship.

Dr. Stetzer also noted that key spiritual questions are different among today's millennials. Previous generations asked about the Bible's trustworthiness and whether Jesus truly rose from the dead. The millennial generation starts with foundational questions. They need to know if God exists. What is He like? Can He be trusted?

Today's millennials can access an abundance of information. Google or Siri can answer any question. The concern is not the lack of information but which information to trust. Millennials have a "prove it to me" mind-set. But Christianity is not provable in the sense of scientific, analytical proof. The compelling proof millennials truly seek is found in an authentic life.

First Peter 2:15 addresses this issue: "For this is the will of God, that by doing good you should put to silence the arguments of foolish people." The arguments will come, but our words alone cannot provide the answers. A life well lived according to the will of God, a life that loves neighbor as self, is what attracts those seeking a better way.

Our goal must be both to share a message that points to God and to live a life that reflects the will of God. When we show concern and compassion over the needs of others, then young people will begin to open up to our message of God's love that is evident and that drives our actions.

## Three Driving Influences

After my conversation with Dr. Stetzer, I (Alex) posed similar questions to Andy Lawrenson, student pastor of Nags Head Church in North Carolina. This church has led in cutting-edge outreach and discipleship for more than two decades. It has regularly been recognized by *Outreach* magazine and other Christian media as being highly effective in evangelizing young adults and maturing them for a life of Christian fruitfulness. Many of Andy Lawrenson's alums have not only walked faithfully with the Lord but have also entered full-time Christian work.

In past years I have had Andy and his team lead sessions at my national "Truth for a New Generation" conferences. One attendee said of his presentation about reaching millennials: "They were the most important training sessions I have experienced in 10 years of youth ministry."

When asked why this generation is considered "less Christian" than past American generations, he noted three driving influences. *The first is the changing influence of the home.* When young people see hypocrisy and misplaced priorities in the lives of their parents, they often will look elsewhere for role models and guidance.

*A second influence is culture.* American culture has moved away from Christian values, negatively impacting those raised in it. For example, Christianity is often not portrayed well in the media. It is not "politically correct" to be a Christian anymore. Social pressure to "fit in" as a Christian is largely absent. In contrast, it is considered more socially acceptable to embrace non-Christian identities and lifestyles that stand in conflict with biblical values.

*A third influence is from church.* For some time, the American church has more commonly been known for what it is against rather than what the church stands for. The church is seen as a negative rather than as a shining city on a hill. With this perception, it is no wonder many do not seek to enter the doors of the local church.

## It Takes a Family to Build a Worldview

Attitudes about life largely are formed at home during a child's early years. Single parents raised many of today's millennials, while others grew up in blended families struggling with difficult situations. Others have parents who worked full-time outside the home and invested little time into their children's lives. Influences from public schools, media, and friends shaped these millennials' worldview, often resulting in negative beliefs and behaviors.

*Influences from public schools, media, and friends shaped these millennials' worldview.*

Andy has also observed changing patterns of church involvement and attendance within the millennial generation. Many divorced parents alternate parenting every other weekend, leading to a different youth ministry every other week for young people. Other families prioritize sports or other activities on Sundays in place of church attendance. Overly busy schedules contribute to declining midweek church involvement as well, so many teenagers (and their families) miss out on regular church attendance and the opportunity to build strong Christian friendships. Thus, their worldviews reflect secular culture more than biblical truth. Students don't grasp the importance of the body of Christ for believers.

## Passing the Baton

Another unfortunate scenario is also common in the shift of faith from one generation to the next. According to Andy, parents have largely failed to "make disciples" of their own children. Instead, parents have depended on the church to be the discipleship influence in their kids' lives. This is not only the fault of the parents, but it also stems from the parents' church background and resulting lack of spiritual maturity. These patterns have simply been repeated in the lives of their own children.

A combination of hope and frustration exists among the current generation. When asked about millennials' impact on politics, the economy, education, and the family's status, Andy explained that social justice drives this generation. Millennials often reveal a deep desire to help others in need and to see all people treated with dignity. While these can be positive traits, they can also translate into positions at odds with biblical Christianity.

For example, social justice should compel Christians to serve the poor and help orphans. However, some in today's generation have invested in activism for same-sex marriage, an issue in conflict with God's original design for marriage and the sexual purity God has communicated in Scripture. The push for tolerance regarding any and all behaviors has led to some championing causes and activities that are in opposition to biblical values.

## A Generation at a Crossroads

Will this generation of millennials experience revival in our nation? Andy's answer sounds more like a question. He shares, "I'm not sure. I have seen student ministries shrink to a core of students who are Christ followers. My hope and prayer is that they will be the generation that is ready for revival in America."

Ultimately only God knows what tomorrow holds for this generation and for our nation. However, genuine revival is built upon lives changed by God and people who boldly share His message with others. Our nation stands at a crossroads, desperately in need of young men and women willing to make difficult choices and stand against sin while standing firm in the faith.

Barna Group President David Kinnaman affirms that "millennials who are Christians claim a deeper, more rooted faith than Christians of previous generations." Based on statistics, he says, "the light of millennial Christians is shining actually brighter than that of Boomer or Gen X Christians."[1]

## Disconnected from the Church

Mark Hall is a third front-line expert I (Alex) interviewed about millennials. Mark has served as a student pastor for 28 years at First Baptist Church in Asheboro, North Carolina. He is a highly respected, beloved figure in student ministry. Many up-and-coming youth ministers and thousands of teens, twentysomethings, and young families have been influenced by his teachings.

When I asked Mark to explain why millennials are less Christian today, he shared, "My sense is that millennials

are less connected to a vibrant assembly of
believers who are hearing the gospel and seeing transformation among individuals in the
congregation."

*Life can feel
overwhelming,
so many give
up trying to live
for God at all.*

Generally the parents and grandparents
of today's millennials had a more authentic
and consistent relationship with the people of faith and
expressed it in their worship and service. Many millennials
raised in Christian homes experienced some noticeable differences. Mark says he has seen some parents living vicari-
ously through their children. For example, dads and moms
who fell short in high school and college try to rebound
through their kids. Some parents were scholar-athletes
wanting their kids to continue the tradition. Millennials
often feel parents push their shortcomings and legacies on
them in more ways than they realize. They feel that they
can't measure up and are never good enough. When Sunday
comes, we push faith and Christlikeness on them. Life can
feel overwhelming, so many give up trying to live for God
at all.

When asked about the failure of parents to influence and
transfer their faith to the next generation, Mark pointed out,
"I think we failed to be transparent in our own faith journey.
We were not 'set apart' Monday, Tuesday, Thursday, Friday,
and Saturday. But we 'looked the part' on Wednesdays
and Sundays. We did not connect the truths and live out
Deuteronomy 6:4. We majored in church-ology and programs instead of making disciples. Instead of storing up

treasures in heaven, we obsessed about biographical and résumé data for better schools and jobs."

Mark noted the significant impact that millennials are having on our culture, not only because of the sheer size of this generation but also based on their values and beliefs. He also commented on millennials' impact on politics, the economy, education, and family status in America: "Millennials are marrying later and may or may not have children. In some cases I see them adopting and helping with foster care situations. But deep down, they want a family. They will move a lot and will never work the sun-up to sun-down hours of their parents and grandparents."

Mark adds, "Many are 'nonaffiliated' in politics and will move away from our dependence on foreign oil and any sort of thought of removing dictators by military action. Educationally millennials will seek out private schools and search for the educational systems that best suit their children's best interests. They get on school boards and are watchdogs when it comes to curriculum and who is shaping the worldview of their children. If they are *Can millennials bring revival back to America?* unhappy with the status quo, they communicate through social media."

I concluded my interview with Mark by asking if he was optimistic that millennials will be the generation to bring revival to America. He responded, "[Christian] millennials love God and accept that Jesus is the Son of God. But they are not in love with the church. They will not give as cooperatively through the church budget as they will a particular cause. They are online givers for the most part but will give where they see 'fruit.' Can millennials bring revival back to America? If we continue to embrace the exclusivity of Christ, maintain authentic relationships, confront pluralism, and preach the gospel, then yes, spiritual renewal will come. Don't expect a breakout event like the old crusades where sporting venues were packed out. Expect it to look more like the church in the book of Acts."

## The Beauty of Jesus

Although the numbers might seem discouraging, there are ways to encourage millennials to keep the faith. There are many reasons why young people may become disillusioned with church, religious organizations, or faith in general, such as mistrust, skepticism, rebelling against a negative experience, pressure from atheist or agnostic friends, or a variety of other influences.

If young people have just a few adults who will come alongside them and encourage them to grow in their faith, there's a much better chance they will remain in the church and be rooted in Jesus long into adulthood. So one or two positive influences can make a world of difference in the faith—and life—of a young person.

Not long ago I (Alex) was asked to visit the friend of a friend who had been arrested and jailed. As a minister of the gospel, I consider it an honor to make these visits. When people find themselves in the deepest of valleys, they are often open to allowing Jesus Christ to become Lord of their lives.

The facility was bleak, with rough gray concrete everywhere and seemingly endless hallways covered in flaking paint and filled with barred cells. Not surprisingly, an air of gloom and hopelessness permeated the place, and this was reflected on the inmates' faces.

This jail had a very small courtyard in the middle of the building, with only a few concrete squares in a dirt courtyard. The dusty ground reminded me of forlorn places I have visited in developing nations. Suddenly I noticed that a small flower was growing up against the concrete wall in one corner. It was the only bit of vegetation in an otherwise lifeless place. Some invisible breeze had carried a grain of pollen over the roof and into this bare, open area within the facility. The bleakness of the surroundings made that one little flower appear even more vivid.

When I think of the challenge of reaching the millennial generation, it reminds me of that flower. The difficulties are there. The ground is uninviting. But in spite of the bondage, suffering, and entanglements that permeate this world, the freedoms we have through Christ seem all the more precious. Jesus is the flower of beauty in the barren, dusty place that is our modern-day culture. We pray that our children will see that beauty and the truth of His power to absolve the guilty imprisoned by sin. May their hearts that are longing to be set free draw near to Him and find freedom in Christ.[2]

# Chapter 4

# HOW THE CHURCH
# IS FAILING MILLENNIALS
# (AND HOW IT CAN IMPROVE)

Traveling to churches across the country, I (Alex) have seen a wide variety of congregations. From churches that meet in steepled buildings with stained-glass windows to those located in former Walmarts, gatherings vary more today than perhaps any other time in American history. Despite this variety across our nation, unprecedented numbers of millennials are finding ways to exit church life rather than join it. Why? Who is to blame for the millennial generation's mass exodus from church involvement?

The answer depends on whom you ask. Older Christians tend to blame younger ones (just as previous generations did). Young adults, including many Christians, have listed

multiple reasons why the church became irrelevant or harm-
ful in their lives. There are problems on both sides, with
churches shrinking and millennials seeking spirituality in all
the wrong places.

Our goal is to help point the way to recovery. The church
is called the bride of Christ and is clearly important to Jesus.
Yet many churches have failed to reach the next generation,
while many millennials have failed to recognize the important role the church can play in their lives. As they seek to
reach their own adult children, parents of millennials will
benefit from understanding the relationship between their
sons and daughters and today's church.

There are three major ways in which the church is failing
millennials. As we unpack these failings, our intent is not to
provide a hopeless message of gloom and doom but to help the
church "be the church" and impact the next generation. We'll
also explore ways churches can become more effective in reaching millennials as they grow into the next generation of leaders.

## Valuing Tradition over People

The first and most notable way the church has failed millennials is by considering tradition to be more important than
people. Many church leadership meetings focus on urgent,
immediate issues: financial concerns, building renovations,
and the next children's program. Unfortunately, praying for
and pursuing young leaders often takes a back seat to what
happens next Sunday.

Two extremes have developed in response to this unhealthy focus on "business as usual." First, some churches have decided to start new ministries or completely "rebrand" the church to appeal to the next generation. "If a fog machine is what the hipster church down the road is using, then we'd better buy one too!" A new Sunday-night service launches, leaders start wearing jeans instead of suits, and everyone expects revival to break out. Unfortunately, this is rarely the case. The unchurched community simply continues as-is and doesn't even notice the new dress code or sign on the highway.

*Two extremes have developed in response to this unhealthy focus on "business as usual."*

The second extreme is an unhealthy change in doctrine. To appeal to more people, some congregations and entire denominations have shifted convictions regarding marriage and even their belief in Scripture as God's perfect, inspired Word. These changes may or may not appeal to those seeking a new church, but they certainly do not please God, the One we are called to ultimately honor. If the goal of the Christian life is to bring glory to God, then remaining faithful to biblical convictions is essential.

## Making Safety More Important Than Service

Another way the church has failed millennials is less obvious than the previous issue, but it is just as concerning. Protection and security became of primary importance to the previous generation. Parents sought to guard against "evil" influences, by restricting their children to consuming only "approved" music or films. Many churches moved out of urban locations and into relatively safer suburbs. Christian schools expanded, as did universities, so many children were exposed to only "safe Christian kids" until young adulthood.

While these efforts were well intended, the abundance of caution led away from serving real needs in local communities. To their credit, many millennials see the importance of social justice as a vital part of life—serving the poor, the sick, the imprisoned, the orphans, the widowed, and the enslaved. Unfortunately, many of these same churches have not prepared this generation for such service, leaving young adults serving through secular organizations because they consider the church irrelevant.

Worse, some have moved beyond Christ-centered causes to support social justice efforts in conflict with biblical convictions. Whether promoting same-sex marriage, pro-choice efforts, complete separation of church and state, or other causes, many social justice advocates who came from the church now support causes either outside the church or opposed to its message.

## Choosing Comfort over Cause and Community

An enormous shift has also taken place because of the rapid growth of the American megachurch. The church became more businesslike, corporate, and organized, seeking to compete with Fortune 500 companies in the pursuit of "excellence." Church leadership conferences have sought speakers from Disney and Twitter to help in building "creativity," seeking to appeal to more people in strategic ways.

*They deeply care about finding a small group of friends they can call in a time of crisis.*

While these types of seeker-friendly churches have helped some people, they have generally left a bad taste in the mouths of millennials. This generation tends toward an anti-corporate mind-set that values informality and seeks family rather than a cool children's ministry for their kids or a fancy logo on a coffee mug for visitors. Young church seekers are just as happy at a 100-year-old church or storefront as a megachurch campus. They couldn't care less about the next building project, but they deeply care about finding a small group of friends they can call in a time of crisis.

In addition, when a millennial American considers a church, he or she is more likely to ask what the church is doing for the poor than whether there is a specific Bible study available on Thursday nights. There is a growing desire to be part of a cause rather than to simply attend a church that is more convenient in terms of meeting times, facilities available, or location. A millennial is more likely to pass five megachurches to attend a new startup with 20 friends who really care about his or her life.

## A Rigid Church

Many millennials have distaste for how rigid church has become. They do prefer a church with structure, but not one so rigidly traditional that they don't have a say. Growing up in the church, for most millennials, was awkward. Much of the feedback we have gotten about their experience with church was that it didn't feel natural to them. They were told church was a place to be free and open, but generally millennials never did fully engage. They kept to themselves.

Some millennials raised in the church have known an old-fashioned, exclusive, and judgmental form of Christianity with a chip on its shoulder. They perceive the older generation as forecasting "gloom and doom" for America's future. They hear preachers warning of the chaos outside the walls of the church. Occasionally they see those same preachers eventually destroyed by moral failings.

A few years ago, Rachel Evans wrote a column for CNN called, "Why Millennials Are Leaving the Church." Here are key reasons that speak to the generational differences defining millennials:

- What millennials really want from the church is not a change in style but a change in substance.
- We want an end to the culture wars. We want a truce between science and faith. We want to be known for what we stand for, not what we are against.

- We want to ask questions that don't have predetermined answers.
- We want churches that emphasize an allegiance to the kingdom of God over an allegiance to a single political party or a single nation.
- We want our LGBT friends to feel truly welcome in our faith communities.
- We want to be challenged to live lives of holiness, not only when it comes to sex, but also when it comes to living simply, caring for the poor and oppressed, pursuing reconciliation, engaging in creation care and becoming peacemakers.[1]

We need to remember that millennials aren't against spiritual things or religious observances. They *are* opposed to a watered-down version of Christianity that emphasizes a whole lot of judging and not a lot of loving. Or as Jonathan Swift put it, "We have just enough religion to make us hate but not enough religion to make us love one another."[2]

## Ten Ways Churches Can Improve Effectiveness

While today's churches have certainly failed millennials in various ways, it's not too late to successfully impact the next generation. God is clearly working to raise up young people who are serving Him. The following 10 recommendations identify how churches can better reach and engage our millennial generation.

## 1. Redefine "Church"

Most of us realize that the church is not a building but the people of God gathered for worship. This gathering can occur at a coffee table or in a cathedral. When we narrowly define church as "the group that meets on Sunday morning at a certain address," we limit the people we reach, including many millennials.

Past church trends have included shifting to varied service times or multiple locations. However, the early church simply met in temple courts (a public outdoor venue) and in homes. If we defined church attendance to include those who gather for worship regularly in homes as well as public locations, we could redefine church to encompass outreach to a broader community.

The Southern Baptist Convention, America's largest Protestant group, has begun implementing a ministry called the 1-5-1 Harvest Program in some states. The idea, taken from church planting in the developing world, encourages an existing church to start one new group to reach five new people over the course of a year, multiplying into one more group the following year. This approach has led to new churches in nontraditional locations, including trailer parks, subdivision clubhouses, and even homeless communities.

## 2. Put People First

To successfully reach the next generation, we must focus on reaching people, not getting people into a building or program. The temptation is to compete with the church down the street or the list of the fastest-growing churches in America, saying we had X-number of people last weekend at X-number of services in X-number of locations. But the church still comes down to people reaching people.

That means becoming passionate about the things that millennials are passionate about, which will naturally lead to a connection.

*We must focus on reaching people, not getting people into a building or program.*

We must be willing to find out the needs and interests of those we seek to reach, and work accordingly. We don't need to compromise our message, but we might need to compromise some traditions along the way to make an impact. For example, some churches now take one Sunday a year to "be church" on a Sunday morning and lock the doors for a day of community service. This can be a great start, but what about the rest of the year?

Reaching out requires embracing diversity. The latest research notes, "Millennials are the most racially diverse generation in American history. Some 43% of Millennial adults are non-white, the highest share of any generation."[3] Our churches should ideally reflect the ethnic composition of our surrounding community. This will take place only when we look at people as family, regardless of any external factor, whether race, disability, tattoos, or piercings.

Look at the example of Jesus. When He arrived in a community, He didn't start a program; He served people. Jairus begged Jesus to heal his daughter. As He was walking toward the house of Jairus, a crowd surrounded Jesus, including a lady who touched His clothing in order to be healed. Jesus could have kept going, but He didn't. He stopped, acknowledged the woman, and blessed her. He did not see people as interruptions but as opportunities to be a blessing. When we view interacting with people as an opportunity to be a blessing, it will no longer matter if the person is a millennial or not; he or she will respond to kindness when you put people first.

### 3. Start Where They Are

Jesus set the ultimate example by leaving heaven to enter humanity and serve among us. When we look to Him for ideas, we realize that to be effective requires going to those we seek to reach. Jesus did not say, "If you build it, they will come." (That was the film *Field of Dreams*.) Jesus commanded His followers to go and make disciples of all nations (Matthew 28:18-20). We tend to look at this command for missionary strategy, but it also works next door and in our own community.

Imagine this: Instead of inviting young adults to attend your Sunday service, go to your local college campus and give out free pizza. A few recruited young adults play some music, a crowd gathers, and a few people share stories of how Jesus changed their lives. You tell people you'll be back the same time next week and do it again. Repeat for the entire school year and see how many lives are changed. You may end up reaching more people on a college campus than in your Sunday service.

This principle doesn't just work on college campuses. You can do the same at your office at work (if they will allow a place to meet). A few guys in Memphis started riding their bikes downtown and passing out burritos to homeless people. The weekly event became so big, they now reach hundreds of people each week and are helping change the face of homelessness in their city (ubfm.net). Who knew burritos and bikes could build the church and change society?

## 4. Translate Your Message

We don't need to change the Bible's message to reach the next generation, but we do need to translate it. Just because you and those you wish to reach both speak English doesn't mean you are communicating. To reach new people, you have to communicate the message in meaningful words and structures others can understand and respond to.

*Explain why the Christian message is important for today.*

We have to realize that many millennials did not grow up in church, and neither did their parents or their grandparents. Their only knowledge of the Bible is as folklore. Many Americans believe that the saying "God helps those who help themselves" is found in the Bible. (Just to be clear, it's not!) They are just as likely to believe in karma and reincarnation as they are to know the real reason for Christmas or the names of even half of the twelve disciples. We must start at the beginning and explain why the Christian message is important for today.

Our message also needs to be the "full counsel" of Scripture. It's easy to tell people to say "this prayer" and you'll be forgiven and go to heaven. Yet we must also honestly communicate that God calls us to live differently if we choose to follow Him. We can no longer live any way we want but instead are called to serve the Lord and be different from those around us. The way of Christ is amazing and filled with love, but it is also difficult and will include many struggles along the journey.

## 5. Accept Millennials as Family

We live in a culture where half of marriages will end in divorce. More than 40 percent of those who are born today are born into an unmarried family. Even those in traditional, two-parent families have often faced abuse or neglect. The great cry of this generation is for family relationships that withstand the ups and downs of life.

Did you know just 26 percent of Millennials are married? "When they were the age that millennials are now, 36% of Gen-Xers, 48% of Baby Boomers and 65% of the members of the Silent Generation were married. Most unmarried millennials (69%) say they would like to marry, but many, especially those with lower levels of income and education, lack what they deem to be a necessary prerequisite—a solid economic foundation."[4]

The good news is that the church is designed to fill this need. When we choose to treat our congregations as families rather than organizations that offer spiritual services, we will attract those longing for brothers, sisters, fathers, mothers, grandparents, and siblings.

Imagine what would happen if every person who visited your church on Sunday received a handshake or hug from every person he or she met. What if every new person was invited to sit by not just one but five or six or seven different people? This kind of overwhelming message of family and love will attract people to church better than any follow-up program or breakthrough in technology. Accept millennials as family and they *will* be family.

## 6. Release Creativity

The average millennial knows at least some computer programming, can build his or her own website, and can put together messages that reach thousands within minutes through social media. Many have amazing skills with music, art and literature, or design. Wouldn't you like to have more of these skills in your church?

Many of the highly creative millennials in your community would pitch in and serve if you gave them a compelling reason to do so. We can no longer be afraid to hand over a project to a twentysomething because he or she "might not be mature enough." If we're honest, we weren't mature enough when we started either. We learn best by doing, not watching.

The solution to a poorly designed church website is already sitting in the pews. The answer to a lack of student-ministry

*The solution to a poorly designed church website is already sitting in the pews.*

volunteers is already prepared to respond. When you remove barriers, the church naturally grows. When the church is healthy, it grows naturally. God controls the pace, but we can implement and support changes that will nurture growth.

## 7. Mentor Each Millennial

Simply put, millennials are open to receiving help. They often don't know how to go about getting it, however. As a church, we are all about making disciples through relationships. We are built for mentoring. If we can become more intentional about creating one-to-one connections between younger and older people in our congregations, we won't have to worry about young people leaving our churches when they grow up. We'll experience deep relationships that keep people close—better than any program in the church.

Mentoring sounds great, but where can we begin? In most churches, leaders of the congregation can set the pace. Typically a leader will mentor one person who then commits to mentoring one other person. Each of us is a "Paul" seeking a "Timothy." Second Timothy 2:2 states, "What you have heard from me in the presence of many witnesses entrust to faithful men who will be able to teach others also." We help another who helps another who helps still another. The goal is not only one-to-one, but also one-to-one for at least four generations of mentoring.

*The process of mentoring will be more caught than taught.*

The process of mentoring will be more

caught than taught. When pastors and church leaders and people in every Bible class share about those they are mentoring, others will want to get involved. Start small, stay strong, and keep investing in the lives of one another in your church.

## 8. Help Millennials with Everyday Life Skills

Most millennials need help in a wide variety of life skills ranging from managing finances to forging positive relationships, from finding jobs to performing basic car repairs.

Skills taken for granted in past generations often are foreign to today's youth. Without the influence of a father, many young men do not know how to interact with other men or how to properly behave toward women. Young men often are not taught the importance of basic caring acts, ranging from confidently shaking hands when greeting another person to holding a door for a woman or elderly individual.

Some millennials have successfully learned these skills, but many others have not. What could your church's congregation do to offer help with basic life skills? Some offer financial literacy classes. Others offer programs for young men such as Trail Life (traillifeusa.com) or AWANA classes that support parents in raising children of character. Some churches offer men's ministry opportunities that include fishing and hunting while women's ministries gather to support each other in various work or life activities. No church can address every need, but every church can help.

## 9. Include Millennials in Leadership Decisions

If a church wants to reach millennials, it's important to include millennials in decision making. We can't assign decisions to the older generation and successfully address the needs of the next generation. We must include those we wish to reach.

This is also true of ministries within the church. To get younger people into the choir, let them choose some music the choir performs. To see more young men leading in the church, put them in charge of something significant. Young women are often maxed out with childcare and working while also leading in the home. To involve young women in the church, offer safe (and free) programs for children while moms and dads attend worship or serve in ministry.

## 10. Send Out Millennial Missionaries

It may seem like a paradox, but to reach millennials, we must plan to release them. This may come as a surprise, but what often attracts young people is the chance to tackle a big challenge. There is little appeal in sitting through music and a lecture on a Sunday morning. But send them into a local juvenile center to serve among incarcerated youth? Now you have their attention. Help with a winter shelter in subzero temperatures to save lives? Finally, something that sounds interesting!

*To reach millennials, we must plan to release them.*

When I (Jason) interviewed David Kinnaman, president

of the Barna Group, he described a new approach to discipleship to win the battle for the hearts of the millennial generation:

First, we need to recognize the efforts of our Adversary, who tries to steal, kill and destroy the good things that are happening in our children's lives. So, in some sense, we have to realize there is a larger context for what is happening and why the struggle is so intense.

Second, we are discipling in a totally different context than we have before—we call it digital Babylon. It's a world of all-access, relational alienation and deep skepticism of authority. So we need better, more holistic means of making disciples. We need deeper relationships and better friendships between generations within the church. We must provide a generation with a richer understanding of cultural discernment, especially via Scripture.

Discipleship in this new context requires a great commitment to developing and mentoring leaders— and to allowing younger leaders real opportunities to shape their churches and businesses. It also requires what we describe as "vocational discipleship," the concept of helping millennials understand their God-given purpose through work and also how to be faithful in the complexity of life's callings.

Finally, discipleship in this context demands that we allow for millennials to have a firsthand experience of Jesus. That's, of course, the beginning and end of our discipleship efforts. We are concerned that Jesus is simply getting lost in the Twitter stream. To a lot of millennials (and older adults, too) He's more like a Facebook friend than He is the creator of the universe who desires intimacy with us.

Each of those dimensions of discipleship that I've just described—meaningful relationships, cultural discernment, mentoring and reverse mentoring, vocational discipleship, and experiencing Jesus—all must be centered around the Bible for it to take hold of young hearts and minds.

The paradox of the millennial generation is that despite the reputation for apathy, many desire to take on truly great challenges to make a difference. They want to be heroic. Millennials don't get too excited about attending the monthly business meeting, but tell a young person you're ready to minister to gangs in your city, and somebody will say yes. Tell the young women in your church you need someone to minister to victims of sexual assault, and someone will make time to show up. The more extreme the situation, the more it appeals to those seeking adventure in life.

I (Alex) know this in part because it happened to me early in my ministry. I was a seminary student eager to use my gift of public speaking to impact others. Instead of speaking at my local youth ministry (which I was already doing), I chose to share the gospel in 50 states in 50 days. At that time, no one had ever done it. This gave me the opportunity to be the first to do something *and* to change lives.

What seemed to be an impossible calling launched the ministry I have lived out since that time. Today much of my ministry is traveling nationwide to share the gospel. In addition, my unique 50-day experience led to many media interviews. Today, I cohost a nationwide radio program and a television show, interviewing Christian experts to influence others. It all goes back to being called to do something considered impossible.

*It all goes back to being called to do something considered impossible.*

Think about it. You may have the next Billy Graham or Mother Teresa or Martin Luther King Jr. in your community. You don't know it yet, but creating and supporting compelling ministry opportunities may be the missing ingredient your church needs to call out the next generation of leaders.

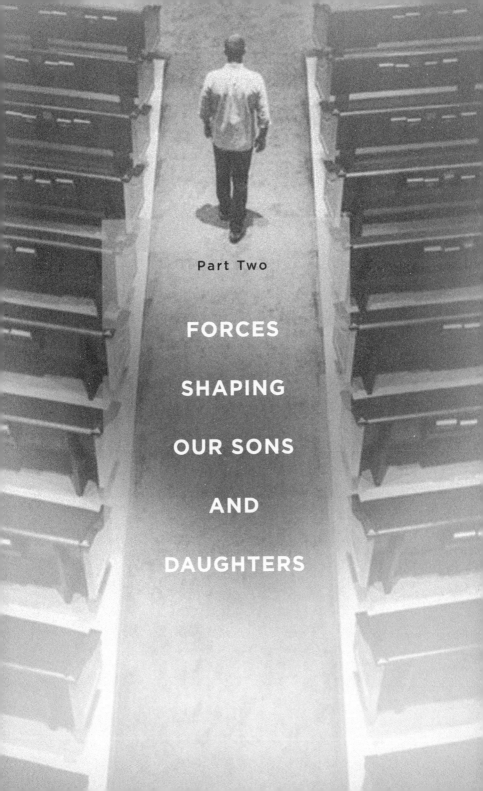

Part Two

# FORCES
# SHAPING
# OUR SONS
# AND
# DAUGHTERS

# Chapter 5

# STRUGGLES MILLENNIALS FACE

MILLENNIALS ARE CHALLENGED in our culture with struggles different from those of their parents. In this chapter, we'll examine leading issues influenced by shifting standards of morality, the dominance of technology, cultural changes, and the decline in our economy. Among these issues, economic decline affects most of our adult children, resulting in a difficult relationship with money for many of them.

Though raised in a struggling economy, many millennials have grown up expecting to start with more and earn more in adult life. Financial literacy has been a struggle for a majority of millennials. A TD Ameritrade survey revealed the following:

- 76 percent of young millennials (ages 15 to 24) said they know little or nothing about how to invest.
- Nearly half (47 percent) of Americans this age believe that a savings account, earning minimal interest, is the best way to prepare for retirement.
- Only 17 percent of those ages 15 to 24 said they feel that the stock market is the best way to grow their money.[1]

A six-month survey among millennials who use Facebook offers interesting data regarding the financial values of this generation. Some 53 percent have no one they trust for financial guidance, while only 37 percent have a financial plan. In addition, millennials are redefining what it means to be financially successful. According to the study:

- 46 percent believe financial success is defined by being debt-free.
- 21 percent believe financial success is defined by owning a home.
- 16 percent believe financial success is defined by buying experiences.
- 13 percent believe financial success is defined by being able to retire.
- 4 percent believe financial success is defined by buying nice things.[2]

Negative fallout from the Great Recession took a toll on millennials in a number of ways. The Pew Research Center notes millennials are "the first [generation] in the modern era to have higher levels of student loan debt, poverty and unemployment, and lower levels of wealth and personal income than their two immediate predecessor generations." While previous generations were, on average, age 26 when they earned the median wage, millennials on average are age 30 before they earn the median wage.[3]

Millennials have responded in a variety of ways. Some have moved back home with mom and dad. Others have struggled with discouragement and depression. Still others remain optimistic, working multiple jobs and using creative means to make rent and other life expenses. Despite a negative financial situation among the majority of millennials, their optimism is often noted as high.

It's important that parents not only gain insight into millennial values regarding money struggles but also discover how your son or daughter can better address personal financial issues. In this way you'll be equipped to better understand and assist your child in positive ways.

## Economic Uncertainty Equals No Jobs

Millions of millennials struggle to find full-time jobs after college. Many are upset that college degrees appear worthless based on the limited job market. With the spike in university tuition and massive student loan debt (1.2 trillion and counting) and with jobs being shipped overseas, the economic mess accelerates for our children and grandchildren.

*Today the numbers of young men and women living at home with their parents have surged.*

The job market is a challenging one for millennials. What does this mean to parents? It might mean adult children are still living at home or parents are paying a child's rent while he or she tries to figure out next steps. Today the numbers of young men and women living at home with their parents have surged. According to Pew Research, about 36 percent of millennial women and about 43 percent of millennial men are still living at home.[4]

You may be nodding your head in frustration, saying to yourself, "I spent hundreds of thousands of dollars for my child to graduate college—and for what? They're not even using their degree!"

I (Jason) had one graduate student tell me how depressed she was about not getting a job. This girl worked hard throughout high school. She prayed, picked, and planned out her college degree at the university of her choice (thanks to the scholarship she worked so hard to get). She went on to get her master's, graduating with high marks. Upon graduation, she landed a paid internship. After the year was up, the company was on a hiring freeze, so that was that. She hasn't found a job since.

How old were you when you moved out of the house? If you are like the average person in your generation, it was probably between 17 and 20. Now if you stayed home to attend a local college, it was probably a wise economic move.

But more than half of millennials don't ever leave home. This phenomenon is known as *emerging adulthood.*

We noted previously that younger millennials (ages 18–28) are still developing mentally. Emerging adulthood describes the stage where most millennials are still developing their independence—professionally, financially, culturally, or prospectively. They are often still finding themselves in their twenties.

We can't tell you how many articles, videos, and books we encountered that champion emerging adulthood. Some very respected experts in family therapy say it's a good thing. They insist that emerging adulthood shouldn't be looked at as an *inhibitor* but rather as a *connector* between parents and their adult kids.

Jen Doll, a journalist from *The Atlantic*, addresses parental concerns about their twentysomethings not finding a career or getting married:

> Earlier generations might have asked, *Why don't these kids just settle down and get married?* Or, *What's wrong with staying at the same company one's whole life?* But those specific concerns are less relevant to today's twenty- and thirtysomethings, who've been brought up to believe that they should have the freedom to choose from options well beyond what their parents were offered. While their parents may worry, this isn't a bad thing, according to the experts.[5]

We are not sold on this line of thought. Earlier, we pointed out that our millennial generation was raised in a culture with too many choices. Remember, parents played a big role in this! Now that these young adults are in their twenties—jobless and homeless with no chance in sight of getting married—where's the motivation to change if mom and dad keep doing the heavy lifting?

Don't get us wrong. Some situations are out of your son's or daughter's control. Living at home or taking out a "loan" from parents may be their only option (temporarily). That can actually become a good *connector* for parents and their kids. But if your millennial has no game plan and you see no movement toward independence, then this live-in situation will only become a dead-end road for the both of you.

Just consider this wisdom from the Bible about personal responsibility:

- "For each will have to bear his own load" (Galatians 6:5).
- "When I was a child, I spoke like a child, I thought like a child, I reasoned like a child. When I became a man, I gave up childish ways" (1 Corinthians 13:11).
- "Whatever you do, work heartily, as for the Lord and not for men" (Colossians 3:23).

Ultimately, it's not good for adult children to live at home with their parents. If they have to, then the arrangement needs to be temporary with fixed agreements and goals before your millennial returns to his or her childhood bedroom. (See the appendix, "When There Is a Failure to Launch," for more ways to help your son or daughter in transition.)

It's important to understand why moving back home is the only good option. You and your spouse need to pray together and determine whether this is a good arrangement. Otherwise, you will be looking after an adult child instead of babysitting grandkids. If you have a fairly good relationship with your adult child, then these conversations may not be so hard. But if you and your adult child are struggling, then pray for wisdom before making any solid decisions.

It's also important to remain sensitive to your adult child during this transition. It can't be easy asking to move back home. Many millennials have gone to school and juggled two or three part-time jobs, yet because of the bad economy, they can't keep a steady flow of income. It's hard—not only for them but for parents as well.

*Many parents have told us that their biggest fear is that their millennial will never move out.*

Many parents have told us that their biggest fear is that their millennial will never move out. One mom, who had three grown children, started taking anxiety pills when her daughter moved back home. She said, "The longer my daughter stays with us, the less chance I will ever be a grandmother."

As I (Jason) write this book, my wife and I are helping close friends walk through this situation. Their daughter returned from a gap year, but now she doesn't know what to do next. Her plans change all the time: one day she wants to move overseas; the next, she wants to become a chef.

My wife received a text from this girl's mom stating that she felt like a failure as a mother. My wife began to pray for her and sent her Psalm 40:1-3 to meditate on:

> I waited patiently for the LORD,
>     and he inclined to me and heard my cry.
> He lifted me up from the pit of destruction,
>     out of the miry bog,
> and set my feet upon a rock,
>     making my steps secure.
> He put a new song in my mouth,
>     a song of praise to our God.
> Many will see and fear,
>     and put their trust in the LORD.

You might find comfort meditating on these words yourself.

These are critical times for millennials. And that's why it is so vitally important that you stay invested in their lives. They need you now more than ever. And remember, you are not alone in this situation. Find other parents who share your concerns. Speak up at church. Surround yourself with a support group of like-minded parents committed to helping each other work through these challenging times together.

On a positive note, today's millennials have unique perspectives and strengths that offer hope for getting through the difficulties resulting from tough economic times. Let's turn our focus to ways millennials can start searching for and seizing opportunities to succeed.

## It Begins with Employment

Using money begins with making money, which means employment. Millennials spell money J-O-B. Yes, stagnant wages have led to more low-paying jobs, but a variety of opportunities do exist. Those who are young also find ways to forge ahead through multiple jobs, side hustles (projects online and offline to make extra cash), living resourcefully to save on expenses, starting businesses, and saving carefully to pay down debt and prepare for the future.

*Many millennials juggle multiple jobs to generate more income.*

Many millennials juggle multiple jobs to generate more income. Often, part-time jobs are easier to find. Since turnover may be high, having another job means there is more than one source of income available to pay the bills. In addition, many millennials view holding multiple jobs as a way to pay down credit cards or college loan debt faster.

Some millennials work a second part-time job for the health insurance. Picking up weekly hours as a barista at Starbucks is worth far more than the low-paying hourly wage because of access to health benefits.

Another positive reason for multiple jobs is that one job may "pay the bills" while the second job might be built around a hobby or passion. For example, one recent graduate works in an office all week, but on the weekends he serves as a whitewater rafting guide, pursuing his passion while making extra cash. Popular online guides and books encourage this generation to blend their expertise with their interests to build jobs that pay at least something toward ongoing needs. Those who are successful seek to launch their personal businesses into full-time careers or *side hustles*.

A side hustle is a supplemental job or project a person does to make extra cash. Unlike an ongoing job or second job, a side hustle may come and go, or spike for a brief time and then take a break, depending on the time of year or season of life. From Uber drivers to projects on fiverr.com (where people do microprojects for $5 each) to selling on eBay or Amazon, side hustles are the back-up plan for many millennials. There are literally hundreds of creative ways to make small amounts of money online for those with the time and technical skills to participate. Millennials with ambition are leading the way in these unlikely, yet growing, fields.

**Millennials may eventually be known as the side-hustle generation.**

Millennials may eventually be known as the side-hustle generation, using whatever creative means are necessary to sell products and services to various clients online and offline, providing paying opportunities unavailable in a downward economy.

## Resourceful Living

From Groupon to AirBnB, millennials are making the most of crowd-sourced living to save money. Armed with only a smart phone, a millennial can book a discounted flight through an app called Hopper, catch a ride with Uber or Lyft, and stay in a spare bedroom with AirBnB, traveling cheaply and in style.

What about saving on rent? Some still opt for traditional roommates. While an increasing number of millennials return home after college to save on expenses, others are experimenting with tiny homes or even co-op living arrangements.

For transportation, those in cities are increasingly turning to bicycles and public transport. Fewer millennials own cars than their Gen-X counterparts, both because of financial realities and a desire to leave a smaller footprint on the environment.

The typical millennial's material needs can be filled quite differently from his or her parents'. There's Plato's Closet, a thrift store for brand names, offering preowned, high-end clothing. With Netflix, Amazon Prime, Hulu, and other streaming services, high-cost DVDs are becoming relics of a past generation. And cable television? Who needs it? A landline phone? Why bother? Pay for music? No thank you. Music is free through Spotify and nearly any Google search. Project Gutenberg offers more free e-books than a person could read in a lifetime. Some even skip the smart-phone data and head to free locations for wifi to save even more.

Budgeting has also become easier through online banking and budgeting apps. Many millennials, contrary to popular thought, actually have a basic budget and try to stick to it.

Fewer are obtaining credit cards, cutting off further debt. More millennials rent than buy homes, and those who do have a car tend to purchase used or lease a vehicle rather than buy new.

While there are still some expenses linked to the above solutions, apps and online tools are becoming the extreme couponing of the millennial generation.

## Starting a Business

Some business experts have shown concern that millennials may be starting fewer businesses than previous generations did. However, the difference is that millennials are starting side businesses rather than structured corporations. Anyone with a laptop can launch a store on Etsy to sell crafts or list services on various websites to earn income on the side.

Because typical millennials realize the up-and-down nature of running a business, many work for one place as a main job while running other projects on the side. This could have complications for some workplaces, but it's a reality that more people, especially millennials, will need to work in multiple ways at any given time.

There are other surprising benefits for those able to start a business from home. Parents can cut back on paying for childcare. Commuters no longer require a costly daily drive. A married couple can share a car. Working from home can save money spent dining out or buying clothes that conform to an office dress code. Combined, these factors offer many additional benefits for those who can find a way to work from home.

## The Problem of Delayed Milestones

A major outcome of the financial challenges facing today's millennials involves traditional adult milestones. For economic and cultural reasons, many of these milestones are occurring later and later. For example, it used to be that high schoolers got their first cars around age 16. By 18 years of age, a person is legally an adult who can move away from home. With families unable to afford an additional vehicle and young adults staying or living at home after college, these milestones are delayed.

*Many of these milestones are occurring later and later.*

When a student exits college with tens of thousands of dollars in student loan debt, the prospect of marriage can be overwhelming. Young adults are marrying later in life and less frequently in general. According to one report, "The median age at first marriage is now the highest in modern history—29 for men and 27 for women. In contrast to the patterns of the past, when adults in all socio-economic groups married at roughly the same rate, marriage today is more prevalent among those with higher incomes and more education."[6]

## Lack of Family Planning

Historically speaking, it was very common for people to marry young. Women were married by 20, and men by 22. Kids came shortly after.

By contrast, today the average age at which millennials

marry is more than five years higher. Half of the babies born from people under the age of 35 are out of wedlock.[7]

You may be a parent reading this right now whose millennial had your grandchild outside of marriage. And it's possible that your millennial and your grandbaby are living with you because the relationship didn't last. Truth is, when two people cohabit and start having kids, their chances of staying together before their first child reaches kindergarten is less than 20 percent.

Allow me (Jason) to provide two real-life examples of this issue. The first involves a student in my church years ago. She was bright, energetic, and extremely emotional. You never knew what you were going to get with her. Her parents were legalistic, always involved when the church doors were open. They were so busy at the church, and with entertaining church friends, that their daughter was slipping into doubt and rebellion. I had many talks and prayer sessions with this family, but in my heart I knew this young woman was going to hit rock bottom.

*"This is not what we wanted for our daughter or for our grandchild."*

In a few short years, she walked away from church and got involved with a group of friends that partied and hooked up often. Eventually this young girl moved in with her boyfriend, an atheist. She got pregnant, and they married a few months later. I saw firsthand what this did to the girl's parents. The outcome was never what they expected for their daughter. "It's a mess," the father told me. "This is not what we wanted for our daughter or for our grandchild."

The other example involves a family who came to me with major problems. The father and son got into some pretty big fights. One fight was so bad that the two of them were arrested. I don't think I ever saw such anger in a father and hatred in a son. This "Christian" family lived with so much bitterness. Everything was an argument with them. It was nonstop. I remember how frustrated I got with this family. Once I even kicked them out of my office because of their childish behavior.

I wish I could say their son got his act together. He never did. In fact, he got worse. He moved out of the house hastily and moved in with some friends. Eventually he hooked up with a girl, got her pregnant, and left her shortly after their baby was born.

These two former students of mine each have a story. They may not be proud of their stories, but the endings have yet to be written. We pray their lives will some-day become stories of redemption.

*In spite of economic and cultural struggles, there remains great promise for the millennial generation.*

In spite of economic and cultural struggles, there remains great promise for the millennial generation, according to author and researcher David Kinnaman. During our inter-view, he spoke about the contributions millennials will have on society:

There are plenty of reasons to believe that millennials will have as big or bigger impact on society than did the baby boomers. Demographically they are huge in numbers, and they are very diverse in terms of ethnicity and belief. They are optimistic about changing the world and are often naive, even overly self-confident in their ability to make that change happen. It's easy to write off millennials because of their apparent narcissism, but remember who raised them. We find that being able to provide meaningful work, a larger-than-life challenge, realistic goals, and relationally oriented communication helps millennials stay connected to the organizations and institutions (such as their workplaces) that they want to change for the better. This idea of mentoring and reverse mentoring (where millennials are an important source of input and leadership) is critical to the success of today's families, businesses, and churches. Just look at the political process: it's very hard to be successful in elections today if you don't have active engagement across various generations, including Boomers and millennials (and Gen-Xers and elders, too, by the way). We need that kind of effective intergenerational partnership within the church now more than ever.

Chapter 6

# UNDERSTANDING WHAT DRIVES MILLENNIALS

We've looked at the spiritual beliefs of millennials, but what about their cultural values? What do millennials consider important and why? By understanding millennials' motivations, we can draw conclusions about why so many of them are walking away from their faith and the church.

Much study has already been invested in understanding the traits of this generation. Corporations desire to know how to better manage young employees. Universities desire to better recruit high-quality candidates. Ministries desire to better evangelize and disciple a new generation of believers. By looking at some of these studies, we can observe characteristics common to this generation. In this chapter, we'll look at eight primary millennial values and how they influence the way this generation operates today.

As we better understand these common values, we can appreciate those that align closely with biblical values, while also standing firm against values that oppose a Christian worldview. We'll also discover which values held by your child may serve as the key to greater understanding and change in the days ahead.

## Value 1: Meaningful Work

The Brookings Institution made an important observation regarding the value of work among this generation. Fred Dews notes that "64% of millennials would rather make $40,000 a year at a job they love than $100,000 a year at a job they think is boring."[1] Research further concluded that millennials desire the following:

- interest in daily work being a reflection of and part of larger societal concerns
- emphasis on corporate social responsibility, ethical causes, and stronger brand loyalty for companies offering solutions to specific social problems
- a greater reverence for the environment, even in the absence of major environmental disaster
- higher worth placed on experiences over acquisition of material things

- ability to build communities around shared interests rather than geographical proximity, bridging otherwise disparate groups[2]

Do you see these traits at work in your own child? Income is important, but meaning is a central motivation for the next-generation workforce. If your child struggles with his or her vocation and keeping a job, it could be because of this very factor. Everyone desires meaning in their work, but for millennials this is essential.

*Everyone desires meaning in their work, but for millennials this is essential.*

This value can be seen in the success of social businesses. These companies dedicate a portion of sales to a particular cause. One familiar example is TOMS Shoes, a company that provides a free pair of shoes for a person in need when a customer purchases a pair of shoes. In fact, 89 percent of millennials expressed that they were more likely to buy from companies that supported solutions to specific social issues.[3]

Many times, those who make such purchases do not do so because the product is superior but because of the good feeling and the positive social feedback received from a purchase that gives back. The same is often true of those who seek to work at such companies. When work pays the bills and helps those in need, it is a win-win for the bank account and the soul.

The Barna Group's research on vocation among millennial Christians also notes:

Churches can deepen their connection with millennials by teaching a more potent theology of vocation, or calling. . . . Vocational discipleship is a way to help millennials connect to the rich history of Christianity with their own unique work God has called them to—whether it's within the walls of the church or not.[4]

Vocation is valuable and meaningful to millennials as well as to Christians in general. When taught and experienced together, millennials can find a work-life mix that connects with faith in powerful ways.

## Value 2: Collaboration

Today's digital natives have worked in a wide variety of teams since preschool. The importance of teamwork rarely needs to be taught to millennials because they have practiced it for many years. From youth sports leagues to the middle school group science project, millennials are often better experienced in working together than their Boomer or Gen-X coworkers.

Collaboration has also drawn millennials to certain companies over others. For example, Google, Apple, and Facebook are often noted as top companies where millennials desire to work. Each of these tech giants is known for their collaborative teams and desire to promote work-life balance.

It is no accident that millennials excel in companies and fields where team environments are key to success.

## Value 3: Staying Connected

Millennials can be accurately described as the world's most connected generation in history. Some 80 percent sleep with their cell phones next to their beds.[5] Nearly 41 percent of millennials have no landline at home, depending on cell phones for communication.[6] Three-quarters have profiles on social networking sites. One in five has posted a video of himself or herself online.[7]

Amazingly, 41 percent of millennials say losing their cell phone would have a greater negative impact on their daily routine than losing their car or their computers. Nearly half of millennials sometimes choose to spend time with friends online instead of driving to see them in person.[8]

Constant connection drives much of the millennial's life. Those who seek to reach this generation will prioritize communications that connect through these means, including websites, social media, mobile messaging, email, chat, apps, and the use of smart devices.

## Value 4: Social Justice

*Another positive value of this generation is the desire to make a difference in today's world.*

We've already seen that millennials desire a vocation that involves meaningful work. Another positive value of this generation is the desire to make a difference in today's world. Nearly every millennial has a cause or organization to promote, somewhere to volunteer, or a place where he or she gives. While their financial contributions may include smaller gifts, their desire to serve is found in personal involvement with charities, churches, and nonprofits that connect with their personal interests. From supporting pet rescue centers to building forest trails to preventing suicide, social justice has become the catch-all term for these good works.

This value can clearly be used for good among today's millennials. For example, if your church has a ministry that sponsors children in Honduras, you'll find young adults who desire to support your efforts. Want to provide clean water in Southeast Asia or fight genocide in Africa? Millennials are all ears.

On the flipside, millennials have two areas where the church can provide assistance. First, many Christian millennials seek to provide help without a concern to share the gospel. In other words, working for better health care in the developing world or fighting human trafficking can be done with no connection to sharing the love of Jesus. As Christians, we should care about and promote both. A healthy balance is crucial for the church to make an impact and create social change.

A second concern involves charitable causes that stand opposed to a biblical worldview. For example, we have been involved in many mission-related efforts, yet we've also been labeled for hate speech by nonprofit organizations that claim to promote tolerance for all people. Just because an organization is a nonprofit or a charitable cause doesn't mean it offers social justice in the biblical sense.

Old Testament prophets proclaimed justice in areas such as fighting poverty, freeing slaves, ending war, and assisting prisoners. Yet these prophets also promoted the holiness of God and called all people to live according to His ways. Our desire to contribute to social justice causes should be consistent with our biblical values. When we serve, we can often effectively do so alongside millennials while promoting a biblical worldview.

## Value 5: Diversity

According to the Public Religion Research Institute, college-age millennials (ages 18–24) are considerably more racially and ethnically diverse than the general population. Fewer than 6 in 10 (57 percent) millennials self-identify as white, compared to 72 percent of the general population. Approximately 1 in 5 (21 percent) identify as Hispanic, 14 percent identify as black, 6 percent identify as some other race, and 3 percent identify with two or more racial categories.[9]

This change in composition has led to a healthier acceptance of various cultures and backgrounds. God created man and woman in His image (Genesis 1:26-27) and all are equal in His sight. However, America's history of racism toward African Americans, mistreatment of women, and discrimination toward non-European groups such as Native Americans and others have made diversity a dark spot in the American church.

On the other hand, Christians have also served at the

heart of changing each of these situations. Christians led the abolition movement, led the women's suffrage movement, ministered among Native Americans, and led the Civil Rights Movement. Today, despite the disparity that exists in local congregations, an increasing number of churches are beginning to reflect the diversity of their communities.

A brief word should also be mentioned about the way diversity is often used in our current political climate. While God creates all people equal, some actions are explicitly noted as sinful in Scripture. While those who advocate same-sex marriage would accuse Christians of intolerance, this issue is not about diversity but rather about the acceptance of a sexual practice Scripture opposes.

## Value 6: Spiritual but Not Religious

The Pew Research Center notes that millennials are the least overtly religious American generation in modern times. It states, "One in four are unaffiliated with any religion, far more than the share of older adults when they were ages 18 to 29. Yet not belonging does not necessarily mean not believing. Millennials pray about as often as their elders did in their own youth."[10]

*College-age millennials are more likely than the general population to be religiously unaffiliated.*

The Berkley Center for Religion, Peace and World Affairs notes, however, that millennials have mixed feelings toward modern Christianity. Approximately three-quarters

(76 percent) of younger millennials say that Christianity "has good values and principles," and 63 percent agree that modern-day Christianity "consistently shows love for other people." On the other hand, nearly two-thirds (64 percent) of millennials say that "anti-gay" describes today's Christianity somewhat or very well. And more than 6 in 10 (62 percent) millennials also believe that present-day Christianity is "judgmental."[11]

Today, college-age millennials are more likely than the general population to be religiously unaffiliated. They are less likely to identify as white evangelical Protestant or white mainline Protestant. Millennials also hold less traditional religious beliefs. Fewer than one-quarter (23 percent) believe that the Bible is the Word of God and should be taken literally, word for word. About 1 in 4 (26 percent) believe the Bible is the Word of God but that not everything in the Bible should be taken literally. Roughly 4 in 10 (37 percent) say that the Bible is a book written by men and is not the Word of God.[12]

According to the Pew Research Center's "Millennials in Adulthood" survey, "This generation's religious views and behaviors are quite different from older age groups. Not only are they less likely than older generations to be affiliated with any religion, they are also less likely to say they believe in God. A solid majority still do—86%—but only 58% say they are 'absolutely certain' that God exists."[13]

This characteristic of being spiritual but not religious can be used for good by those seeking to connect with millennials.

They are generally open to spiritual discussions and practices if communicated without the jargon and stereotypes. In the process, millennials may find the power of Christ and the impact of Scripture for themselves, bringing these spiritual seekers to true faith based on a relationship rather than a religion.

## Value 7: Education

According to the Pew Research Center, millennials are also likely to become the most educated generation in American history, thanks to the demands of a modern knowledge-based economy—accelerated in recent years by the millions of twentysomethings enrolling in graduate schools, colleges, or community colleges in part because they can't find a job. Among 18- to 24-year-olds, 39.6 percent were enrolled in college as of 2008, according to census data.[14]

A US Chamber of Commerce Foundation report adds:

Educators are celebrating the high school graduation rate, which now stands at 72%. This is the highest level of high school completion in more than two decades. Of those graduates, 68% enrolled in college. Approximately 58% of those entering a four-year institution will receive a bachelor's degree within six years.[15]

Our knowledge-based economy continues to drive the demand for both higher education and continuing education.

Millennials are quick to embrace degrees and training certifications that lead to better career opportunities. However, this also has important considerations for churches. Pastors were once looked at as the trained authorities on theological matters. Today many church members hold advanced degrees and can instead research spiritual matters for themselves. Others find answers to their spiritual questions through Google searches instead of a Sunday sermon.

## Value 8: Skepticism

Raised in an age of terrorism and the invasion of Internet privacies, millennials are highly skeptical of government, institutions, and even churches. Two-thirds say "you can't be too careful" when dealing with people.[16] Even the lower number of marriages may be partly attributed to the general lack of trust in relationships.

*Millennials must see faith lived out before they will consider living it.*

This value can have both a positive and a negative effect for those seeking to reach millennials. Negatively, increased skepticism has helped contribute to the rise of the "nones," those who are unaffiliated with any religious worldview. Trust must often slowly be built through caring friendships rather than debate. Millennials must see faith lived out before they will consider living it.

On the positive side, skepticism can lead to better discernment of right and wrong, including false teaching within the church. Jude 1:3 teaches believers to "contend for the faith that was once for all delivered to the saints." Many false teachings persist today, from those that promote works that lead to salvation, to prosperity theology that teaches increased faith leads to greater financial prosperity, to the idea that all religions are basically the same. Skeptical millennials will often perform their own research to determine the truth and not take one person's word as the definitive answer. This practice of discernment, long absent from the church, could lead to an increased popularity for apologetics and the promotion of healthy teaching in local churches.

In this chapter, we've said a lot about what drives millennials. But before we close this chapter we want to emphasize that this generation has much to offer the church and our society as a whole. However, as we've mentioned, many of these values remain unused, misused, or underused unless a parent, church leader, or other caring individual gets involved personally to connect with this highly connected generation.

# Chapter 7

# HOPE FOR A GENERATION

MOST PEOPLE believe everything they read on the Internet.

We hope you are not one of them.

Google the word *millennials*, and millions of results turn up. You'll find out that millennials are the largest generation America has ever seen. That's true. Other links depict this generation as a tech-savvy, multi-ethnic group of consumers unable to live without their devices. That is also true.

What is untrue is the picture painted by many companies, journalists, and bloggers who trash millennials by calling them lazy, cheap, godless, and entitled.

Yes. Millennials can be lazy, but who isn't? Some can also come off as a bit entitled. Some expect to easily move up the ladder without having to put in the time and effort. Again, who hasn't tried that stunt before?

It's clear that millennials as a group have some major issues. We've just laid out valid reasons for concern, yet we don't buy into a depiction of millennials as a "Me Me Me" generation. There is still hope, and we are strong and vocal advocates for millennials, as well as for their parents. We don't believe millennials are going to destroy America. As a matter of fact, we believe millennials are poised to change America for the better. In this chapter, you will discover why there is such hope.

## From Slackers to Engaged Contributors

Scott Hess is considered an expert on marketing to millennials. He has spent most of his career studying the patterns, habits, and behaviors of Gen-Xers and millennials. In his TED Talk, "Millennials: Who They Are and Why We Hate Them," Scott describes the stark differences between Gen-Xers and millennials. Although his talk's title sounds harsh, Scott actually presents an optimistic picture of millennials.[1]

| GEN X (BORN 1960–1980) | MILLENNIALS (BORN 1981–2000) |
|---|---|
| Leaning Back; "Slackers," Cliquish, Judgmental | Leaning Forward; Engaged, Inclusive, Tolerant |
| Anti-Corporate | Commerce Lubricated by Conscience |
| Parents are Authority Figures | Parents are Friends and Helpers |
| Mass Media | Personal Media |

Certainly these labels are generalizations, but they do identify contrasts between Gen-Xers and the generation that followed closely on their heels. For parents who are Baby Boomers, the differences between the world they grew up in and the world their children inherited are even more striking.

Many Baby Boomers came of age during the free-sex era of the Sixties. Some remember Woodstock, even if they were too young to be there. Families were falling apart. In the 1980s, AIDS was on the rise. Violence erupted in the Middle East as Israel was repeatedly attacked. The future looked bleak.

*Millennials have grown up in a society shaped by the Internet and social media.*

Millennials have grown up in a society shaped by the Internet and social media. The future is even more frightening for this generation inundated with threats of global terrorism. This group, not unlike previous generations, is seeking answers. But with so much information in the palms of their hands, profound questions of life and the future are even more numerous and more pressing.

How about the economy? When you were growing up, it certainly had its fair share of ups and downs. At the time of this writing, our economy is in the worst shape it's ever been. With $19 trillion in debt, markets declining, rock-bottom interest rates, and unemployment on the rise, it's no wonder millennials are having a hard time being optimistic.

With this in mind, we need to pray harder and more often for these young people. Help your millennial see that God is a mighty God and that He will see your child through the storm. Psalm 145:4 says, "One generation shall commend your works to another, and shall declare your mighty acts."

In spite of the challenges your millennial is facing with education, career choices, and family, he or she has much to offer to our world by taking advantage of opportunities and perspectives unique to the millennial generation.

## Helpers and Innovators

We have been detailing the leading challenges and troubles of this generation to help you better grasp the situation and therefore embrace biblical solutions. Remember, if and when mom and dad find hope and healing, then, and only then, will that give hope and healing to the millennial generation.

*We have seen firsthand how God is using this young generation to stand for the truth*

Indeed there is great anguish and much to be concerned about with this generation. But it's not all bad. There are two key words that define a growing segment of millennials. Those two defining words are *helpers* and *innovators*. Beyond certain self-involved young people are many millennials who actually care and desire to live lives that count for God. We wish we could tell you all the stories of great and amazing innovators we have met. We have shared the ministry platform with many commendable young men and women. We have seen firsthand how God is using this young generation to stand for the truth and leave everything to pursue God's call for their lives. The apostle Paul said, "I do not account my life of any value" (Acts 20:24), and that same kind of fervor is spreading among millennials.

For instance, consider these millennial Christians who span different sectors of work and ministry:

1. TRIP LEE—A hip-hop artist who has produced several music albums, has gone to seminary, and is a pastor.
2. NABEEL QURESHI—An ex-Muslim from Pakistan who came to Christ and is now an author and speaker for Ravi Zacharias International Ministries.
3. FRANCESCA BATTISTELLI—A contemporary Christian top-selling pop singer who is reaching millions of people with her testimony and music.
4. LILA ROSE—Launched Live Action when she was 15 years old! She is a pro-life national speaker and has worked hard to uncover atrocities that take place at Planned Parenthood.
5. NICK VUJICIC—An international motivational speaker who was born without arms or legs. His ministry Life Without Limbs gives him opportunities to speak in schools, churches, and hospitals.
6. TIM TEBOW—A two-time NCAA football national champion who won the Heisman Trophy as a college sophomore. His brief NFL career led to television appearances and leadership opportunities. Today he is famous for his public display of his faith wherever he goes.

In our travels around the country, we hear incredible testimonies of God's work through this youthful generation. One woman in her late twenties left a high-paying job to serve with Doctors Without Borders. She told us she felt the pull on her heart from God to do more to help others.

A young man came up to us after one of our Stand Strong tours to ask this question: "How can God use me like He is using you guys?" He had been radically saved from a life of porn, drugs, and laziness. He is now reading the Word every day and serving in his church. He has been sharing the gospel with his friends and has seen many of them come to a saving faith in Christ.

**God is not through with this generation.**

God is not through with this generation. We are seeing the Holy Spirit move on these young lives, just as God did with Jeremiah, King David, and Esther. God doesn't need a majority of the millennials. He needs only a few who are willing to lay down their lives for the sake of the call. Too often we look at troubling statistics and conclude that it's over. For instance, surveys galore label millennials the most inconsiderate generation in American history. We're not denying it. We are saying we've got work to do. We must be an example to them and pour into those millennials who "get it." Together we can help those young people who only care for themselves.

God is on the march. He is calling millennials to rise out of their slumber. To shed their self-entitled attitudes and take hold of His calling. The task for parents is to help their millennials focus on more meaningful pursuits besides their circle of friends or latest Internet fad. If you show a young person the joy of helping a group of less fortunate people or the excitement of partnering with an organization bringing clean water to a village, his or her life can change forever.

Too many millennials growing up never really had parents who invested the family's time in service to others. They may have served with a youth group, sent an envelope with cash, or said a prayer for a missionary. But many millennials were never given the chance to be hands-on or experience what it's like to give back. So let's extend grace. We can't just label all millennials inconsiderate, especially not those who are trying to live for Christ.

Earlier we mentioned that the millennial generation has a growing segment of innovators. Some stories about millennial innovators are truly remarkable. On the leading edge of this generation is Mark Zuckerberg, who started Facebook. He is just one of many examples of world-changers, especially in the technology arena.

For Baby Boomers, initially jobs and positions were well defined. Everybody had a clear understanding of what the boss wanted, and they worked hard to fulfill their duties. Then the Gen-Xers came into the workplace. They believed work and pleasure went hand in hand. To get to the top, you had to be driven and remain competitive. In the workplace, many Gen-Xers were creative in planning, coordinating with their MBA friends, and executing their plans in a cutthroat manner. Gen-Xers also made room for women to join corporate teams and led the way for affirmative action.

By the time millennials came on the scene, they immediately connected their feelings to causes rather than brands. Millennials' outlook on the workforce is often defined by a narrative that has nothing to do with stocks and bonds. It has to do with telling stories and bonding with others. It's not about becoming a success. It's about helping people succeed.

*What's special about millennials is their ability to relate to and connect with a person's story.*

What's special about millennials is their ability to relate to and connect with a person's story. So when they work for a company that is more interested in profit than people, they will leave the company. Why? Because selling a product doesn't appeal to them. That's what Baby Boomers did. They were good at manufacturing. Gen-Xers were good at cutting production costs and building a global distribution model. Millennials, with a little help from the Internet, are sharing and connecting their ideas, talents, and resourcefulness to build organizations that make products that serve a greater purpose.

Please don't miss what we are about to say. It just might explain why your millennial can't get, keep, or settle on a particular career. In general, millennials are not motivated to do jobs that don't amount to much. They want to promote causes greater than themselves—to be a part of something instigating change. As Simon Mainwaring said, "The most potentially transformative impact of social media is its ability to encourage brands to marry profit and purpose. The reason brands participate is that such outreach earns those companies social currency enabling them to start or participate in conversations that connect them to consumers in meaningful ways."[2]

*Millennials want to be involved, to help out.*

Often millennials tell us how disenchanted they are with their jobs, not because they're ungrateful but because they don't see the value of the work. Millennials want to be involved, to help out. They have a lot of great ideas and would rather not work solo, but as a team. We need more of this. This gives us hope in this generation.

## Discontent with Current Life Status

Many millennials realize they will never work at the same company for their entire adult life. They cannot count on retiring and receiving Social Security benefits until their seventies, if at all. Inflation and wage stagnation forces more work to achieve the same status as past generations, while higher education continues to add debt without significant promise of return.

Instead of giving up, many are creatively choosing new ways to work and serve their communities. Among the motivated millennials we've met, we've observed that they're highly focused and found creative ways to use today's tools and technologies for good. For example, one young entrepreneur decided to use his business skills to help others with

a unique effort called the unFoundation (theunfoundation
.org). Each month, he and 19 other business owners contribute $100 to a foundation fund. They invite local nonprofits
to apply for funds to improve their community and vote each
month on which one to support. The recipient can receive
as much as $2,000 for their project, and the group gets to
change their community through 12 different agencies each
year. This is only one of many new ways millennials are using
unconventional means to create change.

## Desire for Meaning

As we have stated, millennials want to pay the bills like
everyone else, but this generation is also highly motivated for
impact. A great example can be found in the Trash Mountain
Project (trashmountain.com). Despite its odd name, this
effort is a new nonprofit established by Brett Durbin following a trip to Honduras. They served people literally living
among trash dumps. These people would scavenge for trash
they could resell or salvage to make enough money to support themselves and their families. The experience changed
Brett so deeply that he has started a ministry to serve children
and families living in such situations.

The Trash Mountain Project now serves eight communities in five countries. They have raised more than $5 million
to lift people from poverty and increase education in affected
areas. What begins as a desire for meaning translates into direct
action that now impacts the lives of thousands worldwide.

Brett is not alone in the desire for meaning. Many of the smart phone–obsessed young adults in our nation crave a life that revolves around more than the latest status update or Netflix release. They long for impact. Those who act are finding experiences never attempted by previous generations, often bypassing traditional nonprofit structures or business investments and instead diving headfirst into life-changing activities that fulfill the longing for meaning and meet societal needs.

*Those who act are finding experiences never attempted by previous generations.*

## Direct Impact That Takes Little Time

A great benefit of today's technological tools is that direct impact is easier than ever. Many millennials have a wide variety of friends nationwide and even worldwide through their online connections. Once a decision is made to help in an area, whether to fight cancer or help orphans in India, the tools to communicate with and mobilize others are instantly available.

Gone are the days when an organization would first raise money to build or rent an office, pay for phone lines, send direct mail to large numbers of people, hire a team of staff, and possibly even need a warehouse just to begin. Today's society changers simply start a Facebook page or Tumblr blog and say, "We're ending human trafficking in Miami. Let's meet Friday at 8 p.m. for our first awareness outreach." Others can start a nationwide or worldwide outreach instantly. The same tools used to start the Arab Spring or mobilize events for Black Lives Matter are also available to mobilize those defending the pro-life movement, serving the homeless, or evangelizing unreached people groups.

*Today's world changers are often bi- or even tri-vocational.*

Even better, many of today's social start-ups are what would traditionally be called bi-vocational efforts. In other words, a pastor or ministry leader traditionally served one church or ministry. Those with a smaller congregation could only receive a part-time salary and would work another job during the week. Today's world changers are often bi- or even tri-vocational, working at an office during the week while serving victims of domestic violence or raising money for persecuted Christians outside of office hours. These are efforts every Christian can be part of, literally being the priesthood of believers who are equipped to be the hands and feet of Jesus as the Bible instructs.

The abundance of online information also helps "fill the gaps" for those seeking to launch efforts into new areas. Don't know how to take online donations? Google has a million and one search results for you. Need to know how to install a WordPress theme to create your first website? YouTube has a video or two for you. The limitations have been removed more than ever from those seeking to make a direct impact now.

## Hope in Spite of Hardship

In an interview with Barna Group President David Kinnaman, I (Jason) asked if he was optimistic that millennials will be the generation to bring revival to the United States. His answer reflects the challenges as well as opportunities this generation presents:

*We are actually incredibly hopeful that the conditions for a revival are present.*

In our latest book, *Good Faith* (co-authored with Gabe Lyons), we describe the new moral code, which is essentially the morality of self-fulfillment. People believe that the best way to find yourself is to look within yourself. This stands in stark contrast to the Christian tradition, which teaches that knowing ourselves comes from a fixed point outside ourselves (in Christ as revealed through the Bible). We also show the degree to which our society now views Christianity as either irrelevant or extremist—or both. So, it's much harder to be a Christian today as a millennial than it was in previous generations. The numbers are crystal-clear in this regard.

Despite these trends—and, in fact, because of these trends—we are actually incredibly hopeful that the conditions for a revival are present. This kind of society wherein people are looking to themselves for spiritual truth, where faith is viewed with great skepticism, seems to be a fertile environment for the church to be revived. Even though there are fewer practicing Christian millennials than there were in previous generations, their levels of commitment to the Bible and to evangelism are extremely high. They want to make a difference and to be a part of this great adventure called following Jesus. So for those reasons, and many others, we are confident that God can and will use millennials in the next decade to renew his church and awaken society.

## Developing Millennial Leadership Potential

There is little mystery to the development of millennial leadership potential. Despite many cultural shifts, leadership traits have not changed. A young leader ultimately needs growth in three main areas: character, competency, and chemistry.

*Character* has often been defined as knowing who a person is when no one else is looking. Character deals with values: what an individual believes about life. A young Christian needs to continue to grow spiritually and develop in the character needed to follow Christ. This occurs through personal study of the Bible, prayer, service to others, and time in community with other Christians (Acts 2:42).

*Competency* deals with the actual skills needed in a particular role. A medical professional, for example, requires years of formal education. Yet even an entry-level office administrator position requires certain skills to perform well. Further, each role requires ongoing education to develop *God creates a* an individual into a better team member *variety of leaders* who will influence the organization and *for a variety of* potentially move up to more advanced *places.* roles. Proverbs 19:2 teaches, "Desire without knowledge is not good." Those who seek to stand out as leaders must both desire to do well and work to increase skills needed to do so.

*Chemistry* adds an important third leadership trait to the mix. A person might have solid character and job skills, but relationship chemistry is also vital. We can see this clearly in churches where relationships are key. In one sense, as followers of Jesus we are to copy Paul and become all things to all people in order to reach some (1 Corinthians 9:22). However, most of us have a certain context where we can best serve, whether in a large city or small town, among those who listen to hip-hop or country music, or with people who like to hunt for deer or those who are vegan. God creates a variety of leaders for a variety of places. Choosing wisely which "tribe" we best fit will allow us to use our developed character and competency to best impact others.

If you want to help your millennial child grow into successful leadership roles, here are ten key traits to identify and foster within your own son or daughter.

## 1. Connection

Dr. Seuss keenly writes, "A person's a person, no matter how small." Jesus called it part of the Greatest Commandment:

"Love your neighbor as yourself." To excel as leaders, we must genuinely care for those we seek to impact. Remembering names, showing up on time for meetings, noting special occasions such as birthdays, and including everyone in gatherings and celebrations let other people know you care and want them to be part of your life.

In a culture where families are often fragmented, your connection with another person can make a bigger difference than you think. Investing in a young person for even a few days at a summer camp can result in a lifelong friendship. You don't have to invest for long to leave a memory that goes far. You just have to care enough to connect.

## 2. Motivation

It has been said the world is ruled by the energized. In some ways, this is true. Those who get out of bed and do the hard things that no one else will do are those who will accomplish what no one else will accomplish. While others are playing video games or partying their lives away, encourage your millennial to leave a legacy beyond this life. None of us will look back at life and wish we had watched more Netflix or spent more time online. Instead, we will want to reflect on lives well lived among those who need us.

## 3. Innovation

The partner of motivation is innovation. When we are motivated to do things that help better this world, we will find new ways to innovate and become creative in accomplishing goals. We are made in the image of God, the Creator of the heavens and the earth. He created us to be creative beings.

A great example is found in the story of Apollo 13. With their astronauts stranded in space with a broken vessel, NASA was forced into a situation with a critical deadline and limited parts. Yet the need to save the lives of those on board was so compelling that a way was made and lives were saved. Their high level of motivation led to creative innovation that saved lives. In the same way, we can each seek our Apollo 13–like mission and use it to drive creativity in new ways to make a difference.

## 4. Focus

With hundreds of daily text messages, emails, status updates, and other interruptions, it's no wonder many of us tend to lose focus on what is important. The FOMO (Fear of Missing Out) leads us to abandon focused efforts and respond to every update that comes our way. However, the successful leader chooses to turn off the constant interruptions to focus on the few areas of life essential to long-term success.

To grow as a leader means leading yourself well. Encourage your son or daughter to write down his or her major roles and goals in life. Next, include those time-wasters keeping him or her from success in these areas. A wise goal is to eliminate some time-wasting activities and spend the same time investing in what matters most.

### 5. Encourage

Think about it: If you grow up without encouragement in your home, have a broken relationship or two, and then see the latest news about shootings or terrorism, *how are you going to feel at the end of the day?* Not very good. Even a little encouragement can have a tremendous impact on those living in difficult situations. Leaders inspire through words and actions that help motivate and encourage those around them.

### 6. Continuous Learning

The traditional model of higher education includes four years of college followed by more than 40 years of work. Experts now realize that learning must remain continuous in order to remain effective. This principle is noted both in business and in Scripture. Jesus did not give a seminar and then send the twelve disciples into the world. He lived among them for three full years, teaching them valuable skills that would allow them to effectively serve for the rest of their lives. When we look at life as one big learning experience, we can grow daily, staying motivated to help lead in the lives of others.

### 7. Be a Team Player

So-called millennial "experts" offer conflicting reports regarding how well today's generation works together as a team. From one perspective, millennials are the most connected generation in history, easily collaborating on work projects with engineers in Germany and India or gaming online with friends from Iceland or Japan. From another perspective, the individualistic nature of many millennials can often lead to people who like to "go it alone," choosing control rather than collaboration in many areas of life.

Being a team player means two things: taking responsibility and giving away credit. A good team leader will take responsibility to make sure a project gets done, making the extra contact or checking to make sure nothing is slipping through the cracks. When things go wrong (and they will), the responsible team leader takes the blame rather than pointing to others. When things go well, the team leader shifts the credit to the team, highlighting how each person's involvement led to the project's success.

## 8. Dream Big

Every effective leader must have a driving force toward which all of his or her personal efforts are directed.

The stresses of daily life and long weeks filled with work or school have unfortunately led to little dreaming among many young adults. It's easier to get by than to watch a dream die. Yet dreaming big, when matched with efforts to achieve big dreams, can transform a young person's life and the lives of others.

If dreaming big has been a struggle in your son's or daughter's own life, encourage him or her to kick back with a pen and paper and simply consider some ideas. Ask: What would you like to see different in the world? What could you do to be part of this change? What goal would you like to pursue in life? What would it take to get there? Dreaming big begins when we consider, "What if?" and then begin taking steps toward making these dreams reality.

## 9. Improve Daily

We often overestimate what can be done in a day, but we underestimate what can be done daily. We might not be able to achieve our goals this week, but what if we worked a little toward our goals day by day for the next year? The next decade? The best business leaders are those who study and work each day to improve. The best athletes are those who train and never give up. To be the best at something, you have to be willing to improve at it every day.

The same is true for whatever goals we desire in life. Suggest that your child determine the areas where he or she seeks to grow and then do something each day without giving up.

## 10. Endure

All of the previous nine traits will be limited unless we practice the trait of endurance. Hebrews 12:1 teaches, "Let us run with endurance the race that is set before us," referring to our spiritual lives. The same is true in other areas. Many fail because they give up too soon. Life is not a sprint; it is a marathon.

This is perhaps one of the most difficult lessons for today's generation to practice. We make financial payments from our phones, book hotels with a couple of taps on a screen, and complain when the drive-thru at the restaurant lasts a few minutes too long. The idea of doing any one thing for a long period of time is one of the most difficult challenges facing the millennial generation.

That said, perhaps the one leadership trait that will cause a young leader to stand out from others is the ability to endure. Taking one more step when you're too tired to press on is not a technical skill to learn but a life skill to develop. When we choose to keep going when others will not, we stand out from the crowd and truly become the leaders whom others look to for influence.

## Cockiness to Confidence

Many of millennials exude confidence. Let's not mistake this for cockiness. Despite the downturn in the economy and the massive debt they've accrued in student loans, they remain confident that their future holds a better tomorrow.

That's pretty amazing. Despite economic difficulties and spiritual decline, many millennials still hold on to faith deep down inside. Once we were in an audience with hundreds of millennials, and we asked if they truly believed they will live fulfilling lives as they get older. Over 80 percent of them believed strongly that they would.

*Many millennials still hold on to faith deep down inside.*

We then asked how they knew that. Many said they would

achieve their dreams if they pursued them with passion, hard work, and perseverance. This isn't anything necessarily new. Every generation has dreamers, innovators, inventors, and entrepreneurs. But the thing we get excited about is how many young people are trading in convenience or a self-entitled perspective for lives that will actually do some good.

As we've said before, this should give you, and the rest of us, confidence that this generation is not completely lost. Yes, many millennials still believe that our government should be the breadwinner or that government should pave the way for them. The challenge, therefore, is to invest in those millennials who get it and will confront their generation with bold truth. Proverbs 13:14 says, "The teaching of the wise is a fountain of life, that one may turn away from the snares of death."

Part Three

# STEPS TO
# MEND
# AND MOVE
# FORWARD

# STRENGTHENING YOUR RELATIONSHIP IN STRESSFUL TIMES

To STRENGTHEN YOUR relationship with your son or daughter, it helps to know that the millennial generation is one of the most overwhelmed groups in the nation's history. Many have labeled it America's most stressed-out generation. One study noted the following statistics:

- 30 percent of Generation Y [millennials] struggle to support themselves.
- 44 percent find it difficult to pay for education.
- 40 percent of them are unemployed, yet 79 percent hold college degrees.

- 38 percent are overwhelmed with student loan repayments.
- 51 percent still live at home.[1]

A combination of social pressures, stress, and spiritual struggles has left many millennials exhausted and discouraged. Though generally hopeful, they could certainly use some encouragement during the tumultuous journey of the young adult years.

In this chapter, we'll talk about ways you can encourage your adult child through the various struggles he or she may be facing. You'll also find help and hope for strengthening your bonds during these critical young adult years.

## The Triggers

We have previously noted major struggles common to young adults today. The following seven areas—determined by our interactions with young people and verified in studies— pinpoint common triggers that add to overwhelming stress.

### 1. Career

First, your child must search for a job. Second, the job may or may not be long-lasting, with millennials serving the shortest average job length of any recent generation. Third, young adults are seeking to find positions that have meaning and pay the bills, a difficult combination for a single job to provide. In addition, the rise of technology that goes everywhere can lead to work that goes everywhere. Rather than leaving the office, many people take the office home with them. Calls, texts, and messages stream day and night in some careers, leading to increased stress.

## 2. Calling

A career can be a calling, but a calling is much bigger than any one career. Millennials desire a life that makes a difference. Whether as a nurse, teacher, human rights lawyer, engineer, or minister, a member of this generation often seeks the job that makes the most impact over the job that makes the most money. This tension leads to many difficult decisions. "Should I volunteer at the place I love or try to make a job out of it?" "Do I serve at this after-school program part-time or should I spend more time at a second job to pay the bills?" "Should I spend my money on a mission trip or a vacation, or put it all toward my maxed-out credit card?" Calling shapes life, but determining one's calling causes much stress, especially during the early years of adult life.

*This tension leads to many difficult decisions.*

## 3. Debt

We have noted the important relationship between millennials and money. Many face debt so high that they despair of ever repaying it all. Others feel trapped living at home or in a run-down apartment because of bills. Many young men and women choose to marry later or not at all simply because of economic issues that make joining together in marriage challenging.

## 4. Schedule

The millennial generation averages more than a hundred text messages a day, not including hundreds of tweets, status updates, emails, selfies, and Snapchats on a daily basis. For many, the constant flow of communication seems natural, but it often leads to an unhealthy schedule. A millennial may have a 40-hour-a-week job, hold a side job, volunteer on a regular basis, and have a boyfriend or girlfriend. The 168 hours of the week quickly fill up, leading to late nights and early mornings. Sleep has become a luxury that many millennials crave so much that napping centers have actually started in some cities.

*The constant flow of communication seems natural, but it often leads to an unhealthy schedule.*

These demands on a young adult's time lead to stress, health problems, poor eating habits, and even addictions to various substances to stay awake or cope with life. (Think about the many different brands of energy drinks available these days!)

One *Forbes* article also points out, "Perhaps the most prevalent contributor to anxiety is poor sleep. A study by the University of California at Berkeley found that lack of sleep "may play a key role in ramping up the brain regions that contribute to excessive worrying." Common causes of insufficient sleep include going to bed at different times, not making sleep a priority and spending time on phones or laptops right before bed."[2]

## 5. Relationships

Young adults still often strive to fall in love with the right man or woman who will be "the one" to marry and cherish forever. When a relationship doesn't work out, it can be devastating to those involved. The rest of life can become meaningless, leading to despair and lack of motivation. Add relationship troubles to work, calling, or finances, and a young adult can feel life crashing down in unbearable ways. These feelings of anxiety can lead to unhealthy expressions, including abuse of addictive substances, overeating, depression, or other problems.

## 6. Living Situations

Young adults frequently struggle with living arrangements. Whether at home with parents, renting with a roommate, going it alone, or being married, there is a constant demand to move somewhere better. There is often either home despair or home repair in the works. When living situations turn ugly, life can become difficult 24/7, at work, school, and home—with no place to find rest.

## 7. Education

Often young adults are either in the process of receiving an education at college, paying for college, or trying to go back to college. Those in college struggle to maintain a high grade-point average while making the right "social moves" along the way. Others grow frustrated with not finishing or not being able to find employment that matches the education they invested in. Though millennials have more higher education than any previous generation, they also have to deal with what to do with it, leading to stress connected with career, finance, and relationships.

## Eight Ways to Encourage Your Millennial Child

Now that we've discussed stress triggers, let's see how you can help. Your child may be an adult, but there are ways you can help encourage him or her and make a significant difference.

*There are ways you can help encourage him or her and make a significant difference.*

### 1. Pray Together

We know we are supposed to pray *for* our kids and probably already do. But we want to encourage you to go a step beyond this and offer to pray *with* your adult child. It may feel awkward at first, but there is something special and spiritual about a parent and child who both call out to God for help with one another. Think about it: who else is asking your child to pray together? Maybe no one. If you do, you will form a unique bond with one another and with the Lord in the process.

### 2. Laugh Together

Life is often very serious for our millennial children. One way to lighten things up is to find ways to laugh together. Watch a funny movie or online videos once in a while. Do something silly just for the joy of it. Smile, tell funny stories, and share life together in ways that bring down defenses and open opportunities for additional dialogue about more serious matters later.

## 3. Serve Together

Many millennials enjoy volunteering and giving back to the community. Why not serve together? A weekly or even monthly opportunity to help someone else takes the focus off the stresses in your child's own life (and yours) and puts the attention on those you are seeking to help. This can also help you avoid the dreaded label of "helicopter parenting." Helicopter parenting refers to parents who "hover" over their young children or even their *adult* children instead of allowing them to take responsibility for their own lives. By serving together, your focus is on a third person or group that you both help, not on your child. Serving together also provides common ground for ongoing discussions and interests when reconnecting later.

## 4. Write Encouraging Notes or Messages

Remember those affirming notes you left your son or daughter in elementary school? So does your child. But maybe it has been a long time since he or she has seen one. Take some time to write something inspiring that reflects the love you have for your child. Whether a handwritten note, a text message, or an email, your words hold a power only a parent can provide. Use your words for good, *Watch your child find strength through what you share.*

do it often, and watch your child find strength through what you share.

Scripture is a great source for finding and sharing encouraging words with your child. Some of the following verses can be great ones to use along with your personal note:

I thank my God in all my remembrance of you.

PHILIPPIANS 1:3

Be strong and courageous. Do not be frightened, and do not be dismayed, for the LORD your God is with you wherever you go.

JOSHUA 1:9

Trust in the LORD with all your heart, and do not lean on your own understanding. In all your ways acknowledge him, and he will make straight your paths.

PROVERBS 3:5-6

Let not your hearts be troubled, neither let them be afraid.

JOHN 14:27

## 5. Remember the Good Times of Childhood

As a parent, you can recall stories about your child's early years that no one else knows. Take time to tell that story about your daughter's first steps or your son learning to ride a bike.

Reminisce about that Christmas at grandma's when it snowed or the school play where your child decided to bust out a dance move at the wrong moment. Storytelling has a powerful impact that transcends all cultures. Sharing the good stories from the past can also bring strength to the present moment, no matter what difficult issues your child may currently face.

## 6. Share Pictures or Videos of Special Moments

Strengthen the stories you share when you can pass along pictures and videos of special moments. That vacation to the beach or that birthday party with the sleepover can be relived when you and your child look back at the memories. It's amazing how small details such as the clothing you wore at age five or the furniture in the background of the old house recall memories of earlier times that can encourage your child on a difficult day.

Move beyond your immediate family and share stories from your family history. As children, many kids are uninterested in their great-great-great grandparents, but a stressed-out twentysomething trying to find his or her way might be encouraged to see how the past connects with the present. Family albums or family-research websites such as ancestry.com can help bring together details from the past that can impact today.

## 7. Brag about Your Child in Front of Your Child

When our children are young, we often brag about their accomplishments to other people. It's fun for kids to hear mom or dad tell someone else about the cool things they are doing.

Allow us to share a little secret—this works for grown-up

kids too. Once in a while, speak well of your son or daughter to another person when your child is with you. He may not say so, but it will mean a lot to him and boost confidence in ways other forms of encouragement do not.

## 8. Tell Your Child You Will Never Give Up on Him or Her

This is a big one. You can't simply assume your child knows you care and won't give up on him or her. You have to say it. We dare you to tell your grown son or daughter something like "I hope you know I'm going to love you no matter what. I will never, ever give up on you." These simple words are often difficult to say yet mean the world to your child. Don't just think it; say it!

## Discover Ways to Stress Less

Many factors contribute to the high stress of millennials. So let's conclude with these very practical tips that can help lower stress levels (and they work for parents, too).

First, monitor your sleep. Many Americans lack adequate sleep. Most experts recommend seven to eight hours per night. Many young adults average six hours (or less). Those all-nighters that got you through exam week in college can't be repeated on a regular basis in real life. The best way to have a less stressful day tomorrow is to schedule a full night of sleep tonight and future nights.

*The best way to have a less stressful day tomorrow is to schedule a full night of sleep tonight.*

Second, be careful with caffeine. Let's admit

it: many of us are addicted to caffeine. We like to tell people it's the Christian's socially acceptable drug of choice. Coffee, tea, soft drinks, or energy drinks may be helpful to some degree, but many of us are far beyond the moderation level. Experts suggest consuming fewer than 200 mg of caffeine a day. Check your drinks to see how much you actually consume. You might be surprised. Also, caffeine can take several hours to wear off before your body can fully rest. Each person is slightly different, but don't expect to gulp down a Mocha Frappuccino at 9 p.m. and fall asleep by 10 p.m. Your body will not wind down until several hours later, setting you up for a rough night of sleep (or lack of it) that will leave you dragging the next day.

Third, turn off the tech. The majority of young adults sleep with their smart phones next to them. This has led to trends like "sleep texting" where a person writes back to a text while semi-asleep, with no recollection of it the next day. Turn off all alerts but phone calls at night. If it's urgent, the phone will ring. Television is a problem as well. Many people have resorted to the habit of falling asleep to television, but that is counterproductive. Research shows that blacking out a room from light and sleeping in silence lead to better quality sleep than background sounds or television. Don't fall asleep to noise and video if you want a good night's rest.

Fourth, plan ahead. Much of the stress in our life results from uncertainties such as being late for a meeting, not having directions where you are driving, or not knowing the agenda for an event. A little advanced scheduling can boost confidence and decrease stress more than we realize.

Fifth, watch your diet. There are stress eaters, and then there are eaters who become stressed. Both can be hazardous. *Stress eating* means you turn to food for comfort. Have a bad day? Eating ice cream out of the container will fix it. Rough meeting at work? Grabbing a candy bar from the vending machine will make it all better.

**The truth is that stress eating causes more harm than good.**

The truth is that stress eating causes more harm than good. You might feel better at the moment, but the long-term impact on health is added calories, usually from comfort foods, that lead to being overweight rather than relieving stress.

Sixth, get up and move. Some have said sitting is now the new smoking. The average American office worker might sit seven out of eight hours each workday. That's followed by sitting in the car to commute home, then sitting in front of a screen all evening. The only solution is to get up and move. Consider using an adjustable standing desk at work. There's even a desk treadmill if you're really serious! For most of us, however, our sitting problem can be improved by walking at various times throughout the day and regular exercise outside of the office. Set a timer if you need to, but make sure to get up and move regularly to improve your health and lower stress.

Your child may not need to use all of the tips above, but combined with your determined encouragement, practical changes can bring about major improvements in day-to-day living.

# Chapter 9

# BRIDGING THE GAP

You may not be able to solve the problems your son or daughter faces, but you can encourage your child each step of the journey. With regular encouragement, you can help him or her navigate the challenges of young adult life.

Remember the old dial tone that sounded when logging on to the Internet? That was revolutionary, wasn't it? Think of those words "You've got mail." They made you feel special, right?

Technology has advanced since the humble days of AOL and Hotmail. Who could have imagined downloading music and apps and purchasing items with a tap of the screen on our smart phones? We now have smart cars and smart refrigerators, ovens, and microwaves. It's crazy! You can jump on FaceTime, Skype, or GoToMeeting, and have a live video chat with anybody in any part of the world.

It's amazing to see how advanced we've become. The expansiveness and convenience of social media platforms such as Facebook, Instagram, and Snapchat affect billions of people. Practically everyone is on social media. It definitely plays a major role in shaping *how* millennials interact, as well as pinpointing *what* they like and dislike.

*The hearts of millennials are searching for truth and awakening to real purpose and meaning.*

However, all the branding, messaging, capturing, snapping, and posting has consumed their time and blurred their focus. The barrage of information and attention-grabbing images is nonstop. Social media are a constant source to explore interests and stave off boredom. Yet in the midst of all this noise, the hearts of millennials are searching for truth and awakening to real purpose and meaning.

God is moving on this generation. There is a genuine conviction and desire for authentic conversation, not just over text messages but through face-to-face dialogue. Millennials are comfortable with debate. If you use a tone that conveys you care and express passion for what you believe, they are more likely to keep the conversation alive.

But there is a real Satan, an elite enemy of God who works hard to warp the gifted minds of young people. Whether it's to consume their lives with self-centeredness or lust, or to get them to doubt and reject God, Satan is targeting the minds of millennials. He works to fill them with worldly desires to arouse their lusts; he wants them to give in to the demands of the flesh. Which is why parents need to discover how to keep relationships and meaningful dialogue going with their children.

Up to this point, we have helped you understand the worldview possessed by millennials and have shared our hope that the Holy Spirit will use this generation to bring a revival. We now want to introduce you to powerful ways to bridge the gap with your son or your daughter. This is the prayer of every parent: to have an open relationship with their children and stay actively involved in their lives, as well as in their grandchildren's lives.

*Jesus is your Mediator who will help be the bridge to your child.*

Let's start with a reminder about Jesus Christ, who became a bridge between us and a holy God. First Timothy 2:5: "For there is one God, and there is one mediator between God and men, the man Christ Jesus." Never forget that Jesus is your Mediator who will help be the bridge to your child.

## Sufficient Grace

So mom and dad, how do you communicate with your child? Some parents have a great relationship with their millennial children, sharing openly. Others, not so easily. I (Jason) remember walking into church, and an older woman caught up to me. I could tell she was upset. She told me that she and her husband had their oldest daughter over to the house, and the visit didn't go so well. They tried to talk to her about family, her career, the grandkids—anything to get her to open up about her life. Nothing seemed to work.

She looked at me and said, "I don't know how to have a relationship with my daughter, and it's killing me."

We have had many heartfelt conversations with moms like this one, which is why we have written this book. We want you to find hope and healing as you figure out how to bridge the gap with your older children. But just to be clear, this chapter isn't filled with gimmicks or false portrayals. This chapter—this entire book—is written on the firm foundation that it's God who restores all things. There is nothing too big for God to fix, especially related to broken relationships.

Most of our ministries have been devoted to witnessing and easing the burdens of parents, teens, and millennials. It reminds us of the passage in 2 Corinthians 11:28-29, where Paul expresses his own burdens: "And, apart from other things, there is the daily pressure on me of my anxiety for all the churches. Who is weak, and am I not weak?" As painful as Paul's physical ailments were, his spiritual burdens for the church were far greater. Sound familiar?

*There's not a day that goes by that a parent doesn't think about his or her children.*

There's not a day that goes by that a parent doesn't think about his or her children.

Many of the parents we encounter know this isn't always the healthiest situation, but sometimes they can't help but mentally carry the weight of their children's burdens.

What about you? In what ways are you concerned about your child right now? How heavy is the weight you are carrying for your son or daughter? A dad shared in one seminar, "My wife and I were so worried when our kids hit the adolescence stage. It was tough. There were a lot of arguments and a lot of things we did wrong as parents. But now that our kids are grown, we actually find it way more difficult trying to relate because neither of our kids wants anything to do with God."

What an intense burden for a parent to carry—to be so troubled by the spiritual condition of an adult child. And do you know something? In our travels, we can't tell you how many parents come up to share their heart-wrenching stories about their children, who were raised in the church and are now raising their voices in defiance to God.

Despite the burden you may currently be facing with your millennial, take courage in the words of Jesus given to Paul while he faced extreme hardship: "My grace is sufficient for you, for my power is made perfect in weakness" (2 Corinthians 12:9). No doubt you have looked to this verse for comfort in your own Christian walk. But do you remember what Paul said after Jesus told him His grace was sufficient?

Paul responded to Jesus, "Therefore I will boast all the more gladly of my weaknesses, so that the power of Christ may rest upon me. For the sake of Christ, then, I am content with weaknesses, insults, hardships, persecutions, and calamities. For when I am weak, then I am strong" (2 Corinthians 12:10-11).

*There will be times and situations when God will not remove a difficulty in your life.*

As we see in this passage, Paul faced an unusual affliction that the Lord did not remove (for reasons known to Him alone). There will be times and situations when God will not remove a difficulty in your life. It's not to torture you (though it may seem that way). It's to teach you to endure so that you are stronger in the end. You can't achieve this on your own. Endurance comes by the grace given to you by the love of God.

It's one thing to say you believe in this grace, but it's quite another to experience it. Jesus not only wants you to *know* His grace, but He also wants you to *live* in it. No matter how overwhelmed or weak you or your spouse may feel about the condition of your family, we are here to remind you that the grace of God is sufficient. That means Jesus will adequately give you all that is necessary to gain the satisfaction you desire.

You can rest assured that God is here for you and will carry you through whatever hardships you experience as a parent. Your relationship with God, and the good that comes as a result, is far more important than your relationship with your children. Too often, parents take their focus off God because they are caught up in the web of lies, insults, and endless meandering of their children. But like Paul, no matter how hard the situation may be with a child, be content in the midst of it. God will turn your weakness into strength.

## Turning Stumbling Blocks into Stepping Stones

Paul stated, "We put no stumbling block in anyone's path, so that our ministry will not be discredited" (2 Corinthians 6:3, NIV). Paul didn't create stumbling blocks with those he ministered to—he made stepping stones in his ministry. Paul knew that to reach the Corinthians with the gospel, he had to be extra careful in setting a good example. Likewise, parents must be both sensitive and intentional in being that role model their children need, especially as they get older. They may not take your advice all the time, but they certainly look at your example all the time.

*They may not take your advice all the time, but they certainly look at your example all the time.*

Parents are called by God to be the anchor. They are called to be solid models of truthfulness, honesty, integrity, honor, accountability, and patience. Imagine the impact on a child when his or her father is a walking contradiction. Could your millennial think that about you? Maybe you haven't always set the best example. Rather than beat yourself up or get defensive, look for a way to start becoming a better example for your children.

This reminds me (Jason) of a conversation with a friend at my daughter's soccer game. Our mutual friend, a pastor, was caught having an affair. Apparently it had gone on for years, and he and his wife eventually divorced. A few months later, my friend shared he met up with the ex-pastor's oldest son. The son was very hurt and bitter. When my friend asked this young man about his father, he replied, "I don't ever want to see him again. He lied to us. He destroyed our family. I will never forgive him for that."

Regrettably, my pastor friend allowed lust to be his guide. It cost him not only his ministry but his marriage and the respect of his children as well. All for what? For nothing.

We can't begin to dive into the complex situations parents across the country are facing with their children. We can note, however, some powerful truths to help you get back on track. So, if you want to start bridging the gap with your millennial, first recognize the obstacles in front of you and take full responsibility for any stumbling blocks you put there. Then trust that God will turn them into stepping stones to a better relationship with your child.

## Accept Responsibility

What happens to the head coach when his or her team ends the season 0–16? Sure there is blame that can go around, but the direction (or lack thereof) falls on the head coach, not the players. Coaches will experience losses they had no control over. It's a given. But when the team loses camaraderie and the will to win, that's on the head coach—no one else. Similarly, parents will experience losses with their children. There are going to be times when you make the wrong call. Or your child decides not to follow the coach's directive. But ultimately, the morale of the family falls on mom and dad. It is the responsibility of parents (as with the head coach) to inspire the family to stay on track and to win. That must be on the parent, not the child.

*There are going to be times when you make the wrong call.*

You might have a long list of things your son or daughter has done to widen the chasm between you. Remember, though, that your role far outweighs that of your millennial's. Much of the way your son or daughter reacts toward you is based on an accumulation of reactions they got from you growing up.

This isn't about taking all the blame. It is about taking responsibility for what you have done as a parent and about how you plan to *act* (not *react*) moving forward. Rather than looking at the chaos your millennial has made in the family, ask yourself how much of the chaos stems from your actions? If your family bickers a lot, is it because you and your spouse bicker? If your son or daughter has abandoned the faith, could it relate to a lukewarm faith you may have demonstrated when your child was younger?

All of us would do well to accept responsibility for our actions, and then make things right with our kids.

## Be Patient and Listen

Accepting responsibility is one thing, but finding the patience and willingness to listen in the midst of conflict is quite another. Every argument, every conflict, and every divided family signals a lack of patience. In Proverbs 25:15, Solomon

*Parents who are the most impatient happen to also be defensive and argumentative.*

conveyed, "Patient persistence pierces through indifference; gentle speech breaks down rigid defenses" (MSG). The persistence of patience will overcome any insistent defiance. That's how powerful patience is.

We have found that parents who are the most impatient happen to also be defensive and argumentative. Whenever one of their children questions or challenges their authority, they lose it. They get defensive and turn everything into an argument. Before you know it, all the family members are arguing with each other. Why? Because the parents in that family lack patience.

As a pastor, I (Jason) have had many conversations with men about their anger and lack of patience in the home. A few years ago, I wrote an open letter to a group of accountability partners about my own struggles with patience. Here's an excerpt from that letter:

*One morning, as I knelt in prayer before God, my heart was suddenly gripped with intense conviction. The conviction I was experiencing didn't have to do with a lack of faith or something like that. It had to do with my impatience and shortness with my children.*

*Normally, I am a patient person but for some reason, I'd developed a moody tone with my children. As I pressed God further to reveal this sin in my life, He began opening my eyes to the hidden selfishness in my own heart, and showed me how my sin was damaging my relationship with my children. The thought of my children feeling like their dad is always frustrated with them brought me to tears. I never want my children to feel I don't have time for them, or that they're a bother. I want my children to know I love and cherish each one of them.*

*I knew right then and there that if I was to become a better dad, I needed to humble myself before God and repent of my sin. And so I did. I asked the Lord to forgive me of my impatient heart and of my selfish ways, and sought the Lord to make me a better dad for my children.*

If you find yourself struggling with impatience, then you need to desperately seek what the Word of God has to say about patience, and allow the Holy Spirit to empower you with the self-control needed to overcome anger and bitterness (see Proverbs 19:2; Galatians 5:22; Ephesians 4:2-3). Impatience will never lead you to peace. It will only bring more strife and anger. However, when you live out patience, it will produce joy and peace in your life.

I (Jason) was on the phone with a father of two college-aged daughters. He described the oldest as opinionated and, at times, argumentative. His youngest is the complete opposite. She is quiet, reserved, and nonconfrontational.

After this father explained the difficulties he and his wife had with their oldest daughter, I shared 1 Corinthians 4:20-21:

"For the kingdom of God is not a matter of talk but of power. What do you prefer? Shall I come to you with a rod of discipline, or shall I come in love and with a gentle spirit?" (NIV).

You see, this father had allowed his daughter's disrespect to get the best of him. When she wouldn't listen, he'd raise his voice and remind her that he was the parent. When she ignored their rules, he would threaten to take away her car or stop paying for college. It wasn't about his right to discipline his daughter. Of course he had that right. The issue was the father's tone and attitude. When I pointed that out, he quickly admitted that he was an impatient guy, especially when his daughter was disrespectful. He expressed how he and his wife were finding it difficult to correct their daughter and teach her respect. At one point he even said, "Come on. It's not like I can send her to her room."

**You set the tone by setting a good example.**

He's right. Parenting an adult child is tough. You sometimes feel powerless. But I want to emphasize: *your tone is far more important than your inability to send your adult child to his or her room.* Every time you encounter a situation with your millennial that might get confrontational—you must be the mature one. You set the tone by setting a good example. And you can't set a good example if you don't have patience.

So if we expect to bridge the gap with our children, we must pray for patience and learn to become better listeners. This is indeed a tall order, but parents can take comfort knowing that God has given them all the tools necessary to achieve peace and joy in the family. If you don't like to be in conflict with your kids, how do you suppose God feels? God doesn't want to see His children divided. Remember what Jesus prayed in John 17? That His children would be united.

Thus, the more patient and open you are to listening to your millennial, the more biblical, thoughtful, and diplomatic you will become when dealing with your adult child (see Galatians 6:1-5). Remember, you can't always *take control* of their bad behavior, but you certainly can control your own behavior.

Take the apostle Paul, for example. In 2 Corinthians 12:19-21, he gives intimate insights into his ongoing battle with believers at the church of Corinth. He writes:

> Have you been thinking all along that we have been defending ourselves to you? It is in the sight of God that we have been speaking in Christ, and all for your upbuilding, beloved. For I fear that perhaps when I come I may find you not as I wish, and that you may find me not as you wish—that perhaps there may be quarreling, jealousy, anger, hostility, slander, gossip, conceit, and disorder. I fear that when I come again my God may humble me before you, and I may have to mourn over many of those who sinned earlier and have not repented of the impurity, sexual immorality, and sensuality that they have practiced.

When reading this passage, did you get a sense of what Paul felt for the Christians at Corinth? Did you notice how he

*Parents are constantly dealing with sin-related issues with their children.*

defused the situation by not getting defensive with them? Paul humbled himself and admitted he was afraid to find them back in sin. This certainly frightened Paul, but instead of growing impatient with them, he chose to be longsuffering toward the Corinthians.

How true is this with parents? Parents are constantly dealing with sin-related issues with their children. They are tired, scared, and often so overwhelmed that they want to give up. Even the apostle Paul felt this way. But he didn't let his doubts get the best of him. Instead, Paul's attitude was to face whatever he needed to face. And if the Corinthians were participating in sin, then he would not overlook it but rather confront the sin and offer a love that (he hoped) would restore them to God.

The same applies for you, mom and dad. Part of bridging the gap with your millennial is to confront his or her sin, but to make sure you suffer along with your son or daughter. This is certainly never easy, and it requires a lot of prayer and fasting. To help you navigate this journey, we've laid out five biblical truths to embolden you.

- Pray for wisdom (James 1:5; Proverbs 2:3-6).
- Show compassion (Psalm 77:9; Colossians 3:12-16).
- Express understanding (Proverbs 3:5; Romans 3:23).
- Listen and be patient (Proverbs 14:29).
- Take the yoke of Christ (Matthew 11:29-30).

If you seek to apply these biblical truths in your daily life, you will see some amazing results. Not only will your approach and demeanor start changing (for the better), but your son or daughter will notice as well. And that's a good thing.

## Show Some L.O.V.E.

Some parents deal with issues rooted in lack of laughter, openness, and failure to intentionally value and encourage their children. That's why in the Jimenez house, my wife and I (Jason) came up with the acrostic LOVE to capture what every member of the family needs regardless of their age or personality. We are always looking for ways to laugh together, be open with each other, and value and encourage one another.

*Find ways to make your home and your relationship with your millennial fun.*

This reminder can help you and your spouse be more sensitive to the needs of your millennial and become more intentional in fulfilling the mission to restore your family to LOVE.

- *Laugh.* Your home has to be a place of laughter. If everything is serious and moody, your family will struggle to communicate and share together. But when your family shares moments of humor and laughter, barriers break down and it's easier to talk about sensitive matters. Proverbs 17:22 says, "A joyful heart is good medicine, but a crushed spirit dries up the bones." Elsewhere, Proverbs 15:13 reminds us,

"A glad heart makes a cheerful face, but by sorrow of heart the spirit is crushed." Did you catch that? A key ingredient to bridging the gap with your millennial is to enjoy laughter together. Don't be a sour patch. Get out of your comfort zone and find ways to make your home and your relationship with your millennial fun. Laughter is good medicine. It shows your son or daughter that you not only enjoy life but also enjoy spending time with him or her. Some of our greatest memories involve laughter.

- *Open.* Some families find it difficult to be real with each other. Parents can initiate change by being open with their millennials. It's good when parents are transparent with their children, especially when their children are adults. It opens the door to new opportunities to share with your son or daughter as a friend. Sometimes these opportunities come unexpectedly, providing great times to share the lessons you've learned and the forgiveness you've received in Christ. Remember, if you don't open up, neither will your millennial open up to you. So if you normally have a hard time being vulnerable, get over it. Be open with your children. Otherwise, you will lose the opportunity to speak into their lives. Romans 12:18 says, "If possible, so far as it depends on you, live peaceably with all."

- *Value.* Every member of the family needs to feel valued. Several tips to show you value your child: 1) involve him or her in family matters; 2) ask him or her for opinions or feelings about issues and situations; 3) appoint a role for each family member to play during family gatherings, special events, and holidays); and 4) express gratitude to your child for the contribution he or she provides in this role. Make sure to affirm him or her in front of the family. As Philippians 2:3 says, "Do nothing from rivalry or conceit, but in humility count others more significant than yourselves."

> *Be careful when speaking truth into your son's or daughter's life.*

- *Encourage.* This is a no-brainer, but it definitely is something every family can improve on. Lecturing doesn't equal encouraging. So be careful when speaking truth into your son's or daughter's life. Parents need to seek out the heart of their child (no matter the age) and look for ways to speak encouraging words to him or her. First Thessalonians 5:11 says, "Encourage one another and build each other up, just as in fact you are doing" (NIV). One of the greatest things you can do to show love to your millennial is by being his or her greatest source of encouragement.

You can never go wrong with putting some more *LOVE* into your family. If you desperately seek God to change your heart and daily apply the wisdom provided by God and from this chapter, you can begin to build a lasting bridge to the heart of your millennial child.

# Chapter 10

# HELPING YOUR CHILD BOUNCE BACK FROM TOUGH BREAKS

JOHN WAS AT a coffee shop with friends when I (Alex) ran into him. "How's college going?" I asked.

He looked up from his iPhone. "Hoping to go back again soon."

"Sorry," I awkwardly answered, not sure where to take the conversation next. "What are you doing now?"

"Still working tables at night," he said. "Not the best, but at least it's something."

"How's your family?" I asked, trying to quickly change topics.

"My mom's great," he replied. "She still works a lot, and I don't see her that much at the house."

John was clearly still living at home, despite working part-time, having a couple years of college, and sporting the latest smartphone.

"You been working out much?" I knew he had been into sports in high school.

"Not much anymore. Still gaming with my friends, but not much time for sports these days."

We said our good-byes, and he returned to his friends.

My discouraging conversation with John is one I wish I could say was rare. Unfortunately it's all too common.

Half of today's college students don't graduate. Whether they do or not, many are unemployed or underemployed while carrying tens of thousands of dollars in student loan debt. Increasingly, American young adults stay home or move back in long after the high school years (as many as 80 percent[1]). How can we help our millennial children bounce back when life doesn't unfold as they had hoped?

The answers are not easy. There are ways, though, for parents to assist as their young adult children pursue a rebound. Both experience and Scripture offer several principles that can help millennial children excel as they enter true adulthood.

## Embrace Responsibility

The number-one deterrent we see among young adults who struggle to mature is their inability to accept personal responsibility. The "problem" is always the economy, the government, the culture, the church, the weather, their family, their friends, their health, or some outside factor. Yes, these areas can influence our lives in significant ways. However, every person faces adversity. We can either give up or grow up.

*Instead of changing the situation, many simply complain, while doing nothing to change their futures.*

Many children have grown up with mommy meeting their every need, teachers giving grades that were not really earned, and coaches awarding trophies to every person who showed up to play. Without a parent or other caring adult to teach kids not to blame others for their failures or status in life, the finger pointing continues into adulthood. Instead of changing the situation, many simply complain, while doing nothing to change their futures.

A vivid example can be found in today's college sports. In the past, an athlete would never confront a referee to complain about a call or question a coach's decision. Today you can't watch a football or basketball game without athletes pleading their cases to officials about calls that "weren't their fault."

One shining exception: the Army-Navy football game. This long-standing rivalry is a glowing example of what it takes to change the lives of our young adults. These young men play with heart—and without complaint—from the opening kickoff until the final seconds. Why? They have been trained to accept responsibility for their actions, to respect authority, and to play according to the rules of the game with no excuses.

This problem is not recent but can be seen in the relationship of the first humans in history. When Adam and Eve chose to disobey God, He confronted them regarding their actions. Their first response? Adam blamed Eve: "The woman whom you gave to be with me, *she* gave me fruit of the tree" (Genesis 3:12).

**If you want to help your young adult grow in life, begin by accepting responsibility.**

Eve answered, "The *serpent* deceived me" (Genesis 3:13). Their problem worsened as they failed to accept responsibility and chose to blame others.

If you want to help your young adult grow in life, begin by accepting responsibility, first for yourself, then for your child.

Our children, whether younger or older, learn responsibility by observing our lives. The first way to teach responsibility is through *example*. If we are responsible for our actions, our children are more likely to be responsible as well. If the dirty house is someone else's fault, society's problems are the government's fault, and problems at work are the company's fault, you may need to adjust the way you talk and act in order to be a stronger role model for your child.

## Reject Entitlement

The abundance of *free*—free music, wifi, e-books, websites, or even unlimited texting—has led to increased expectation. Millennials feel entitled to things that past generations had to earn. Too many of today's young adults expect a free ride and paid college tuition or believe the government should provide money for housing, health care, or employment.

What happens when the promise of prosperity is stripped away? The Great Depression left people financially devastated, but what they lacked in resources they made up for in determination and ingenuity. They were the original "do it yourself" society—using whatever they could get their hands on. As a result, the Silent Generation worked hard, wasted nothing, and expected their children to do the same. The Boomer generation that followed experienced one of the most abundant times of financial success in American history—likely because of the resilient attitudes and lives of their parents.

People in developing nations often display a similar attitude. Opportunities exist for those willing to pursue them. A child in a developing country may be the first in a family to pursue a high school diploma, learn another language, or start a business to build a better future. A person's highly motivated drive can arise from going without and having to pursue opportunities in spite of obstacles.

*In our culture, young people grow up with every tool at their disposal.*

In our culture, young people grow up with every tool at their disposal, feeling no internal drive to work hard to improve education, family, or vocation. Instead, a sense of expecting without earning leads to future problems when these expectations do not reflect the reality of adult life.

## Choose to Change the Situation

It's important for young adults to realize that blaming leads to inaction, while taking responsibility leads to efforts to improve. Ultimately the problem is not how many young adults are leaving the church or choosing irresponsible lifestyles—it's the need for both you and your millennial child to follow God and mature in life.

This will look different in each situation, but the key is to make better choices. Setting an alarm to get out of bed at a certain time is a start. If your child is looking for a job, spending eight hours a day searching for jobs instead of playing video games or consuming other media should be a priority. Need to get back into college? Start making calls. Fill out forms. Figure out the steps you need to take and begin.

Some shining examples already exist. People in tough situations decide to rent out a spare bedroom using Airbnb or sell unneeded items on eBay or at old-fashioned garage sales, while others find online side jobs to help pay down student loans or credit card debt. This is the way to move forward: using today's tools to our advantage rather than settling for the current status.

*We can set an example by the choices we make in our own lives.*

As parents, we can pray for such change, encourage these changes, and even assist our children toward positive choices. Further, we can set an example by the choices we make in our own lives. As we do, we can expect progress. Proverbs 14:23 teaches, "All hard work leads to profit, but mere talk leads only to poverty" (NIV).

## Look beyond Today

As Christians, we are taught to live with an eternal perspective. God will not ask what kind of car we drove, what brand of shoes we wore, or what latest device we had. He will be more concerned with how we treated our family members and how we helped people around us. Small acts of kindness done repeatedly will result in a legacy we can look back on without regret.

This perspective, however, is difficult in a give-it-to-me-now culture. Society pushes the latest and greatest, version 7.1 as better than 7.0, and the cult of "new" over actions that affect eternity. When we shape our worldview to align with Jesus' teachings, we find a different reality: the way we treat people matters most. What we do for "the least of these" is more important than fantasy football or shopping at that trendy outlet. We are called to look beyond today.

Looking beyond today involves family. Marriage has typically been an important part of adult life. Once a person chooses to get married, the chances of living with his or her parents diminish significantly. Encourage your millennial to look beyond today and consider what it will take to lead in a family as a husband or wife. Ask him or her: What do you need to do today to someday successfully raise children of your own? Looking at life from this perspective can motivate powerful changes.

## Value Learning over Entertainment

Much of today's technology is geared toward entertainment instead of education. The same tools that can save lives in the medical field or help us better understand Scripture are primarily used for gaming or posting pictures of our latest meal.

The way we spend our time reveals what is important to us. In the past, we might be concerned when a church was overly focused on its sports teams and recreational activities. Now we find entire church small groups built around fantasy sports, video games, or other activities that simply don't contribute much to building the Kingdom of God. And while a "God at the Movies" series at church isn't evil, the obsession with television, films, and media in place of education among believers is alarming. We can use our technology and media to learn or to lust, to educate ourselves or to entertain. Our goal must be to control our technology or it will control us. In many cases, it already does.

Video games used to be primarily purchased by middle school boys. Today, gaming is larger than the movie industry and caters to every age segment, from preschool learning tools to M-rated games complete with nudity and profane vulgarity. As games have grown up, the gamers have not. One of the best decisions today's young men, in particular, could make is to unplug the gaming system and spend the same amount of time doing something to improve one's life. And with the average teenager spending the equivalent of a full-time job each day on media, a person can quickly move from online gamer to an online entrepreneur, online college student, or digital missionary, changing lives and growing in the ability to provide for his own needs and help others.

## Endure during Dark Days

Yes, life is hard. Even if we choose to accept responsibility, change our situation, look at the future, and learn rather than be entertained, we will still find the process difficult at times. In fact, life will likely become more difficult rather than less difficult. The Bible does not tell us obedience or maturity will result in an easier life. Instead, we read, "All who desire to live a godly life in Christ Jesus will be persecuted" (2 Timothy 3:12). This doesn't sound like fun, but it's a truth more real than much of today's reality television.

Just because something is difficult does not mean we should avoid it. Most of life's important milestones require struggle—getting an education, working in a vocation, building a marriage, raising children, volunteering at church, helping those in need—all of these activities involve work, frustration, and many dark days along the way. But just because these areas are difficult does not mean we should not try. Imagine if Martin Luther King Jr. had chosen not to lead the Civil Rights Movement because he thought it would be too difficult. How would India be different today if a once-young woman we now know as Mother Teresa had decided it was too tough to serve the poorest of the poor? Because they said yes, millions of lives and the course of history are different today.

*Often at the end of our rope we fall into the palm of God.*

Your child has that same potential. It requires enduring through the ups and downs of life. There will be setbacks, health problems, broken relationships, and perhaps addictions to fight or layoffs to overcome. Yet the God who created us for great works can bring us back from the deepest of pits to accomplish His plans. Often at the end of our rope we fall into the palm of God. He is holding on when everything falls apart. He will never leave or forsake us. We can endure through the tough times because we have a God who is tougher than the darkest moments life can throw our way.

## Beyond "I" to Him

In the lifetime of today's millennial generation, the focus has shifted to an "I"-centered culture. With regard to personal devices, first it was the iPod, then the iPhone, then the iPad. Today there is "smart" everything, from the smart phone to the smart watch to smart wearables and smart appliances. Every piece of tech revolves around making you a better, faster, smarter, stronger, safer, and more satisfied you.

But the focus on "I" and smart devices tends to put the

focus onto self, leading to a "selfie" culture with no Jesus in the picture. He calls us to deny ourselves, take up our crosses, and follow Him daily. Imagine Jesus with one of today's smart phones. Do you think He would take a picture of each miracle? Would He film His exorcisms to post on social media? Would He blog about what He ate today and the fact that 12 basketfuls of leftovers remained after His prayer and meal for thousands? We seriously doubt it.

Jesus came not to be served, but to serve others. The God of creation left heaven to help those who would ultimately put Him to death. He was and is the ultimate example of humility for a culture consumed with self. His life, and death, should convict each of us to ask deep questions about the way we live today, including the following:

- Whose approval am I really seeking?
- Whose agenda am I really trying to fulfill?
- Whom am I really trying to make happy?
- Am I looking out for those less fortunate and in need?
- Am I making the tough choices to grow and mature in life?
- How closely do my priorities match God's priorities?
- When I look back at my life, will I be thankful for how I lived today?

The answers to these questions can often be found in the small choices we make each day. To rebound from our difficult situations in life, we cannot blame or remain the same.

*To rebound from our difficult situations in life, we cannot blame or remain the same.*

Our goal is to take responsibility for our lives and work hard to make our situation better.

There was a photo floating around the Internet some time ago of a child doing his homework under a streetlight in the Philippines. He had no home, but he was motivated to do something to improve his life. As children, we often have a resilience that says, "I can make the future better. I can change the world." As we grow up, life's disappointments often lead us toward apathy—causing us to give up on the one thing that can propel us forward.

God doesn't see us as failures. He sees us as we see that child under the streetlight. We are His children who can rise up from where we are to live for His purposes and accomplish great things. We don't need much. With God, we already have everything we need.

## Starting the Conversation with Your Child

As a parent, you may be wondering where to start this discussion with your own child. These helpful suggestions show you where to begin.

1. Meet with your child alone. Get a time away from screens and work schedules to really focus together for a period of time. It could be as simple as the kitchen table or as big as a weekend getaway. The

goal is to have a special time away from the norm
to discuss important issues in life.

2. Set the tone. Express your intended outcome at the
   start. You can simply say, "I know things haven't
   worked out as you had hoped. I'd like to talk about
   how we can work toward making things better."
   A clear purpose can help keep the conversation
   on track.

3. Admit your failures. Make sure your child realizes you
   are there to be part of a team rather than just telling
   him or her what to do.

4. Ask about your child's concerns. Before giving advice,
   consider asking your child what he or she thinks
   the issues are. "What are you struggling with right
   now? What are some of the things you want to do
   differently?"

5. Share your desire to see progress. For example,
   "I know you're frustrated your college plans didn't
   work out. What are some of the ideas you've been
   thinking of trying now?"

6. Suggest options based on the discussion. Maybe your
   child really wants to move into his or her own place
   but doesn't know where to begin: "You've said you've
   wanted your own place but aren't sure where to start.
   What if we looked at some apartments together this
   weekend to figure out what it would take?"

7. Plan a time to reconnect and to monitor progress.
   Don't let your time together be only a one-time

*The goal is progress, not perfection.*

meeting. Express to your child how much you enjoy the time together and be sure to have regular follow-ups to build momentum.

Every person is different in his or her rate of change or ability to move forward. The goal is progress, not perfection. When you show your love and support to help your child move forward with goals, it can provide the added encouragement needed to make the difference. Failure is not forever, but love is!

## How Parents Can Lead Millennials to Community

When your kids were younger, the parenting roads were smoother. The signs were pretty straightforward, and signposts swiftly passed in the rearview mirror. Before you knew it, you were traveling down the roads of adolescence. Traffic jams were the daily norm, unwanted delays were expected, and construction signs were posted everywhere.

The trip of adolescence was long, arduous, and stressful. Yet, despite the long setbacks and delays, roadblocks and dead ends, you eventually found your way.

Now your son or your daughter is behind the wheel. Independent. Choosing his or her own route. Which is driving many of you crazy (pun intended). You constantly ask, *Where are you going? Why won't you ask me for directions?*

The truth is, your adult child isn't always going to ask you to jump in and show the way. There will be many twists and turns, and dark roads that your son or daughter will take (or has taken) that weren't mom- or dad-approved. It's terrifying not to know where your millennial is headed.

But take comfort. Though you may not be able to predict every path your millennial will take in life, there is, however, a destination he or she seeks. That destination is community. It is a goal that will help your young adult grapple with life's challenges and bounce back from life's toughest breaks.

In these uncertain days, it may feel as if both you and your millennial are traveling down paths marked *Destination Unknown*. This can be scary and exhausting. Rather than letting it get you down, focus on how you can get into the car with your millennial and together arrive safely at the destination called *Community*.

## Building Community Starts with Marriage

Years ago, when I (Jason) was a pastor at a local church, I ran into a woman who worked downstairs. I said my hellos and kept walking. She called my name. I turned around to see if something was wrong.

She ran up to me frantically. Just a few months back, she had shared about her son and how well he was doing in college. He had always been a great student and even considered becoming a missionary. But now something was terribly wrong. When her son came home for spring break, he told his mom and dad that he was an atheist. She was shocked.

For the next year, I tried helping the family, but their college son never came back to Christ.

I remember how defeated the parents felt. Over and over they would explain their efforts to raise their kids in a Christian home. They spent hundreds of thousands of dollars on private Christian education and stayed involved in as many activities as their kids were in. But as I talked with the parents, I kept noticing something. The couple argued all the time. When he would start to say something, she would interrupt him. When she would speak, he would correct her, which led to even more arguing. It was nonstop.

Why do I bring up this story?

I bring it up because if you want to get along with your millennial, you have to first get along with your spouse. Given the divorce rates and remarriages these days, I'm sure it's going to be very difficult for some of you.

Some of you are divorced and have very little (or no) communication with your ex-spouse. Some of you have been married a long time but were never on the same page when raising the kids. Now that your children are grown, it's a moot issue.

Others of you are divorced and remarried. Which means you have stepchildren in the mix—and that can make things a bit more complicated.

The rest of you are still happily married and finding more ways to relate and get along with your adult children. Good for you!

Families these days are very different. Some are more

complicated and messy than others. But
the fact remains that God expects parents
to strive for togetherness and be a united
front in the home. To have a rock-solid
marriage and be on the same page in their
parenting. *It's really hard to get along with
your millennial if you can't even get along with your spouse.* No
matter how hard you try, it is impossible to keep your marital
problems from interfering with your parenting. Work things
out with your spouse. Do whatever is necessary to save and
restore your marriage.

*God expects
parents to strive
for togetherness
and be a united
front in the home.*

Marriage is the centerpiece of the family. When the marriage is strong, the family will be strong. But if the marriage
is weak, the family will be weak. If the marriage is in trouble,
the family is in trouble. The problems you have with your
millennial may easily be related to past and present troubles
in your marriage.

If things are really bad in your marriage or between you
and your millennial child, seek help from a godly couple,
accountability group, or from a biblical counselor. The Bible
says, "Where there is no counsel people fall, but in an abundance of counselors there is safety" (Proverbs 11:14). Added
guidance will give you the support needed to work through
major issues between you and your millennial. Don't neglect
this. Get the help you need. Because in order for parents to
build their relationship with their millennials, they need to
first and foremost have unity in their marriages.

## Community without Hypocrisy

Recently, I (Jason) was at church, and my good friend and pastor, Alex Kennedy, preached a convicting sermon called "Rejecting Hypocrisy and Pursuing Integrity." He taught from a passage in Matthew 23, where Jesus rebuked the hypocrisy of the Pharisees. If you know this passage, Jesus' message isn't just for the religious leaders of His day. His "woes" apply to every one of us.

Hypocrisy destroys authentic community. We all know that it's impossible to have real community if the people you are trying to build relationships with are hypocritical. Yet too many Christians would rather wear their masks and ignore their responsibility to care for and attend to the needs of others.

Unfortunately, we are living in a time when most Christians are not truly experiencing community among their brothers and sisters in Christ. To them, church doesn't feel like family. To these millennials (who were raised in the church), church seems as if it's a judgmental and hypocritical place. Growing up, their pastors seemed uptight, fake, and self-involved.

That's why I appreciate Alex Kennedy's candor and want to share a portion of what he had to say about himself. Not just as a pastor, but as a father as well.

One of the joys and terrifying thoughts for me is the reminder that in my role as a pastor, shepherd, leader—and as a husband and a father—is the power

and the joy God has given me for goodness, to be
a positive influence through the Word of the Lord
and through shepherding. At the same time, I have
the power and the ability to do great harm: if I were
to do something really stupid through a hypocritical
lifestyle or walking out in willful sin that would be
exposed to my family or this church. The ability that
I have for legacy at home and at church is humbling.
So with that sobriety of thought and that awareness
that none of us are above anything, listen with a
heart of humility, saying, *Oh God, I want to live a
life that honors you, that brings You glory. Even in my
brokenness.*[2]

We all know how we feel about hypocrites. We don't like
them, yet we all have played the part at one time or another.
It is sobering to consider the example we set and the legacy we are leaving for our kids. This thought should convict each parent to examine his or her own
life for hypocrisy. Parents ought to heed
1 Peter 2:1, which says, "So put away all mal-
ice and all deceit and hypocrisy and envy and
all slander."

*What would
community look
like if Christians
everywhere put
away hypocrisy?*

Think about it. What would *community*
look like if Christians everywhere put away
hypocrisy? For starters, it would be genuine. Which is exactly
what millennials are in search of. They don't want to be a part
of an institution that says one thing and does another. They

want to belong. No child, no matter the age, wants to be at odds with others. Especially with his or her parents. God intended the relationship between a parent and child to be a bond of unconditional love, support, and acceptance. "As a father shows compassion to his children, so the Lord shows compassion to those who fear him" (Psalm 103:13). Thus, to have community with others is to have compassion for others.

So if there is any hypocrisy in your life, or masks that you are wearing, now is the time to remove them. Now is the time to start practicing authentic faith that has the ability to radically improve your community with your millennial.

## Community without Compromise

Paul David Tripp is a renowned marriage and family expert. He has published some remarkable work on parenting and other enriching topics. In *Awe: What It Matters for Everything We Think, Say, and Do*, Tripp talks about how parents often fail to see the big picture. He writes:

> I am convinced after talking with hundreds of parents that most parents lack a big, overarching vision that guides all that they do with their children. Sure, they want their children to believe in Jesus, and they want their children to obey, and they hope that they will have athletic and musical ability along with a good education, marriage, and career. But at the street level, they're just reacting to whatever comes at them

on a particular day. Yes, they may say and do many good things with their children. Yes, they are sincere about their children's spiritual life. And yes, they work to enforce a set of rules to shape their children's behavior. But it is a reactive system. The problem with reactive parenting is that is lacks a big picture, which enables parents to interpret what is going on in the hearts and lives of their children and thus target the significant heart issues that are really the focus of all good and successful parenting. This inadequate vision leaves these parents with a neat system set up to control, regulate, and conform the behavior of their children. Now if all you do is control the behavior of your children when they are in the home with you, then when they leave your home, they will have nothing. When they leave home and no longer have that system of control over them, their love will go where their heart has been for a long time.[3]

This is so true. Too often parents miss the big picture because they miss the heart. It's easy to get so busy setting rules and regulating behavior—that you miss "the overarching vision" of parenting. With this in mind, we want to encourage parents to break free from certain negative patterns in order to build community with their children.

What action steps can parents take to help their children find community, even if they are struggling with faith or have abandoned it altogether?

*The heart should be the main focus—not behavior.*

First, parents need to avoid *overreacting*. Overreaction plays a big part in compromising community. Parents can get so wrapped up in the behavior of their child that they miss the heart. *The heart should be the main focus—not behavior.* The heart determines a person's behavior. Jesus said in Matthew 12:35, "A good person produces good things from the treasury of a good heart, and an evil person produces evil things from the treasury of an evil heart."

I (Jason) will never forget an older gentleman who told me to always seek to win your child's heart. That was some good advice. My wife and I are constantly reminded that we aren't to shape our kids' behavior so much as we are to cultivate their hearts. Paul Tripp reminds parents that

> there is a battle raging in the lives of young people, but it is not the battle of biology. It is an intensely spiritual battle, a battle for the heart. This is exactly what Paul wants us to beware of as he exhorts Timothy not to let his heart be controlled by evil desires. This battle is not unique to millennials. It takes a certain shape during the millennial years, but it is the battle of every sinner.[4]

Every time you speak to your millennial, think of it as a deposit into the treasure box of his or her heart. Solomon said it well: "Gracious words are like a honeycomb, sweetness to the soul and health to the body" (Proverbs 16:24). In another proverb, Solomon said, "A word fitly spoken is like apples of gold in a setting of silver" (Proverbs 25:11).

We can't tell you how many times we've had conversations with millennials who tell us they wish their parents would extend more grace and understanding. Parents need to stop *overreacting* to mistakes and start *responding* to their millennial with love and grace. As you seek to get along with your millennial, don't lose sight of the big picture. Don't get caught up in the weeds by trying to get your child to behave a certain way. If there is one thing millennials hate, it's parents jumping all over them for every little thing they do. The more you speak graciously to them, the more you will sweeten their souls.

Second, being *overprotective* will compromise your chances of building authentic community with your millennial. As difficult as it is, you must learn to surrender your child to God so that he or she is allowed to fail and face the consequences of personal decisions. Trying to take control of your millennial's life will only drive him or her further away.

Unwise parents try to *fix* everything instead of allowing God be the *Fixer* of everything! These parents are burdened and emotionally unstable because they are carrying their kids' problems and interfering in their lives.

The next time you try to step in and be the fixer-upper parent, just remember this: *When I interfere, my child will not persevere.* Can you say that out loud? *When I interfere, my child will not persevere.*

When your millennial was a child, running interference

was necessary (for the most part). But not all the time. Parents who have a history of running interference in their children's lives, even into adulthood, reveal a few things. One, they don't trust God. If they did, they wouldn't parent with so much fear. Two, they have a hard time giving up control. If they didn't, they could let go more easily. Three, they lack a proper understanding of grace. If they extended grace, they would be less stressed and argumentative in their parenting.

*Interference is not what your son or daughter needs, nor is it what you really want.*

If this, in any way, speaks to how you've attempted to get along with your millennial (through interference), please—put an end to it. Interference is not what your son or daughter needs, nor is it what you really want. At the heart for both you and your child is the desire to establish a relationship of mutual respect. But when your millennial feels as if you're too *institutional*, and not *relational*, then he or she is less likely to engage.

One young man describes his parents' behavior as "running surveillance" on him. In his late twenties, he feels that no matter what he does, his parents know about it, question it, and want to discuss it. He says, "I want my parents involved in my life, but not if they're going to control it."

Millennials who are never given the opportunity to be responsible can't learn responsibility. In the words of Abigail Van Buren, "If you want children to keep their feet on the ground, put some responsibility on their shoulders."

Third, being *legalistic* will inhibit your relationship with your millennial. Far too often, parents make it more about the rules than they do a relationship. This is a big mistake. Children should not be made to feel they are only loved and accepted if they follow a set of rules. That's not how God loves us, nor is it a precursor to salvation. Therefore, legalism should never be a form of parenting Christians pursue.

Fourth, *unrealistic expectations* will not only hinder community but will also obstruct your child's self-confidence. When parents set expectations too high or demand too much from kids, it sets their children up for failure. Avoid making your millennial feel like the underdog because your expectations are too much to handle.

Fifth, *restlessness* destroys community with your millennial. Think of all the times you criticized your kids for not doing what you told them. I (Jason) am guilty of this. When I am restless, I take it out on my family. When we become restless, we might become frustrated with our spouse, or nitpick our kids, or get irritated easily when things don't go right. Restlessness is a silent killer. It will destroy us, our families, and harm our kids well into their adult years.

When your children were younger, did you walk alongside them if they had doubts and questioned their faith? Did you seek your child's heart and allow him or her to begin conversations that challenged his or her faith? Did navigating the winding roads of adolescence with your child make you restful or restless?

When parents look back at these pivotal moments of their children's lives, they often remember how busy, stressed, and restless they were. When your children were younger, they fought for your attention. Yet if your mind was cluttered with things that needed to get done, you may have neglected to give your family members much-needed attention. When restlessness goes unchecked, it breeds frustration and isolation, as it did for David: "I am restless in my complaint and I moan" (Psalm 55:2).

**Please, give your burdens to God.**

When we, as parents, are restless, it's because we are not resting in Jesus. Please, give your burdens to God. Let Him renew your strength and give your soul the rest it desperately needs.

Sixth, and last, *insecurity* can prevent a parent from having an authentic relationship with a millennial child. The lingering question *Do my kids think I did a good job raising them?* haunts most parents (if they are being honest). Most parents would agree that parenting has stretched their faith more than anything else in their lives.

I (Jason) was teaching a class on parenting, and several well-respected couples were sharing struggles they had as parents. One mother said that her insecurities had prevented her from being the mom God called her to be. She didn't believe she was a good enough wife or a good enough mother. Eventually depression set in. She could no longer function throughout the day, so her responsibilities as a wife and mother came to a standstill. After several years, her husband couldn't take it anymore, so he filed for divorce.

This is what insecurity will do to you if you let it. This mother's insecurities destroyed her family and destroyed her life. That's not what God wants for us. He doesn't want your insecurities to inhibit your life and risk destroying your family. He wants you to find your security in Him and gain the confidence to be the mom or dad He wants you to be.

God wants you to boldly say, as did King David, "I have set the LORD always before me; because he is at my right hand, I shall not be shaken" (Psalm 16:8).

Part Four

# WINNING
# BACK
# YOUR
# MILLENNIAL
# CHILD

Chapter 11

# THE POWER OF
# A PRAYER MAP

HAVE YOU EVER FELT the urgency and burden to pray and intercede for your children? Of course you have. Sometimes it's just a little feeling, such as thinking about your child throughout the day. Other times your heart is heavy, and you feel as though something isn't right. Panic sets in, and before you know it, you're freaking out. Some of the worst thoughts rush through your bewildered mind: *Is my daughter safe? Did my son get in a car accident? Maybe I should check to see if he or she needs any help.*

Immediately you grab your cell and send a text. Seconds later you send another one. No response. So you call. After the second ring you're thinking the absolute worst has happened.

You're in a panic, and your patience is fraying. Finally, you get a text. *I'm fine. What's wrong with you?*

After all the panic, worry, sweating, and tears: *That's it? I'm fine? There was nothing to worry about? It was all in my head?*

Yep. When parents have these terrified moments, it's usually all in their heads. If this has happened to you, don't worry. You're not losing your mind. It happens to the best of us, and the best thing to do in these moments is to pray. Intercede on your child's behalf and pray for his or her safety and well-being. In her classic book *The Power of a Praying Parent*, Stormie Omartian writes, "As you pray for your children, you will find it to be an unending habit of your heart. Being able to positively affect your children in prayer will keep you in close contact with them and actively involved in their lives, even after they leave home. And

**It is prayer that moves the heart of God.**

it will continually contribute to your joy as a parent!"[1]

One of the joys of prayer is that it's not limited. You can pray for anyone at any time. So even if you and a son or daughter aren't speaking right now, or you're having a difficult time communicating—talk to God about it. Pray specific prayers and blessings over the situation or with your child. In the midst of your longing to reconnect with your distant child, make the time to connect to God on your child's behalf. It is prayer that moves the heart of God.

Take it from a man of God, one we attempt to emulate: E. M. Bounds. He had such an extraordinary prayer life.

Reading through his sermons and books has inspired us to strive to be diligent and effective in our own prayer lives.

In his classic book *The Necessity of Prayer*, E. M. Bounds penned these profound words:

> Importunate prayer is a mighty movement of the soul toward God. It is a stirring of the deepest forces of the soul, toward the throne of heavenly grace. It is the ability to hold on, press on, and wait. Restless desire, restful patience, and strength of grasp are all embraced in it. It is not an incident, or a performance, but a passion of soul. It is not a want, half-needed, but a sheer necessity. The wrestling quality in importunate prayers does not spring from physical vehemence or fleshly energy. It is not an impulse of energy, not a mere earnestness of soul; it is an inwrought force, a faculty implanted and aroused by the Holy Spirit. Virtually, it is the intercession of the Spirit of God, in us; it is, moreover, "the effectual, fervent prayer, which availeth much." The Divine Spirit informing every element within us, with the energy of His own striving, is the essence of the importunity, which urges our praying at the mercy-seat, to continue until the fire falls and the blessing descends. This wrestling in prayer may not be boisterous nor vehement, but quiet, tenacious and urgent. Silent, it may be, when there are no visible outlets for its mighty forces.[2]

*Developing intimacy with Jesus ought to be your number-one priority.*

With so many demands in life, prayer has taken a back seat. Common excuses for failing to pray include being too busy, too tired, or too distracted. However, more than anything else, parents don't pray often because they lack faith. They do desire to pray, but it's a struggle to invest time to cultivate intimacy with Jesus. Developing intimacy with Jesus ought to be your number-one priority. If you want to have the faith to pray and experience a life of answered prayer, then surrender your life completely to God.

We titled this chapter "The Power of a Prayer Map" because it is vitally important that parents receive guidance on digging deeper in their prayer lives. It's not only for themselves but also for the sons and daughters they want to lift up to God.

Before we unpack ways to pray for your millennial, let's start with a few essential prayer elements found in the Bible.

## Praying to God

Don't you just love worship experiences? They make us feel connected with God. But have you ever considered *what constitutes a worshipful experience?* Does it require flashing lights and loud music? Does it involve an inspiring message preached by a celebrity pastor? Not at all.

Across the country millions of people flood satellite church campuses and big concert venues weekly, expecting a worshipful experience. But too often these eye-catching performances take our focus off God. To be blunt, we should not need multi-media performances to draw close to God. Let's set aside flashing lights and loud music and focus on what matters the most: *our prayer life with God.* There are no gimmicks when it comes to a one-on-one relationship with God. God doesn't play on our emotions. He wants us to draw near to Him and spend time in His holy presence. This is what constitutes a true worship experience.

## A True Worship Experience

In 2 Chronicles 30, we find the amazing story of Israel and Judah participating in one of the most memorable worship experiences in Jewish history. King Hezekiah sent couriers throughout Israel and Judah with the message to "return to the Lord" (v. 6) and "come to his sanctuary" (v. 8). We are told that many responded to the invitation (v. 13). Never before had Israel and Judah gathered together with such repentant hearts. The altars were removed (v. 14), the priests and Levites were consecrated (v. 15), and the Passover lamb was sacrificed (v. 15). The people were having such an incredible experience that the feast was extended for another seven days. During the final week the people sacrificed 2,000 bulls and 17,000 sheep as offerings to the Lord (v. 24). Talk about a lot of sacrifices!

In the midst of the worship, consecration, and animal sacrifices—one special element was needed to culminate this historic experience. That was prayer. The Bible says, "Then the priests and the Levites arose and blessed the people, and *their voice was heard, and their prayer came to his holy habitation in heaven*" (v. 27, emphasis added). As grand as King Hezekiah's feast was, it's fascinating that prayer is mentioned as the one thing that came into God's "holy habitation." It wasn't the *big production* or the *elevated performance*. It was the simple act of prayer that grabbed God's attention.

**Prayer is also considered to be an offering to God.**

Why is that? Because prayer is also considered to be an offering to God. In Psalm 141:2, David cried out to God, "Let my prayer be counted [made ready] as *incense before you*, and the lifting up of my hands as the evening sacrifice" (Psalm 141:2, emphasis added). Interesting. Why would David describe his prayer as "incense" to God? David believed his prayers were offerings to God. In those days the priests would offer sacrifices to God on the altar and burn incense (an aromatic fragrance) in the tabernacle. The smoke from the incense would fill the tabernacle as a lovely aroma. Thus, David is likening his prayer to a sweet-smelling aroma offered to God at the evening sacrifice (see Exodus 29:38-42; 30:7-8).

**It is an act of worship— a sacrificial offering.**

This is a central insight into prayer. It's not enough to say your prayers in hopes God hears them. Prayer is so much more than that. It is an act of worship—a sacrificial offering. This image of prayer can change the way you look and think about prayer.

Consider your prayer life through the years. How many

rotten prayers have you offered to God? How many selfish requests and flippant prayers have you made in your life? If you ask most of us that question, all we could do is bow our heads in shame. But David no doubt had his fair share of foul prayers. That's why he continued to pray: "Set a guard, O LORD, over my *mouth*; keep watch over the door of *my lips*! Do not let my *heart* incline to any evil" (Psalm 141:3-4, emphasis added).

### All-Access Pass

One of the most incredible privileges we have as children of God is our all-access pass to His holy habitation.

Just think: you can come before a holy God anytime you want. And the more you spend in God's presence—the more habitual holiness will be in your life. Psalm 96:9 states, "Worship the LORD in the splendor of his holiness; tremble before him, all the earth." Hebrews 12:14 reads, "Make every effort to live in peace with everyone and to be holy; *without holiness no one will see the LORD*" (emphasis added). So as you journey through prayer before a holy God, make sure you pursue holiness in all that you do. Otherwise, your prayer life will cease to exist.

## Praying God's Will

Prayer is all about having the faith to say, *not my will, but Your will be done*. Anything less is a faith*less* prayer. The Bible makes it abundantly clear that without faith it's impossible to please God (Hebrews 11:6).

Therefore, when you come before God—you don't come to Him in your name. When you pray, you pray in the eternal and holy Name that is above all names—Jesus Christ (which literally means "The Anointed Savior"). It is the Name by which we are saved (Acts 4:12). It is the Name that trumps all other names. Many Christians talk about praying God's will—that's good, but it's quite another to *submit and accept whatever His will is.* Yet that is what Jesus himself did.

*Prayer, according to Jesus, not only requires an obedient heart, but also a heart of humility.*

Prayer, according to Jesus, requires not only an obedient heart but also a heart of humility. Remember the account in Luke 18, Jesus' parable of the Pharisee and the tax collector? You would think the Pharisee would know how to offer prayers whereas the sinful tax collector would not. Verse 11 says the Pharisee *"stood by himself,"* while the tax collector, in verse 12, *"stood at a distance."*

This means that the Pharisee stood praying to himself, while the tax collector knelt in prayer to God. Jesus points out that the prayer of the Pharisee was self-righteous and proud, while the prayer of the tax collector was humble. And in the end, Jesus says the tax collector went away justified, not the Pharisee.

Why? Because God receives the humble prayers, not the proud and pompous ones (Luke 18:14). When you come before God with a spirit of humility and brokenness, He will respond to you in mighty ways.

Andrew Murray beautifully articulated the quality and grandeur of humility:

> Humility is perfect quietness of heart. It is to expect nothing, to wonder at nothing that is done to me, to feel nothing done against me. It is to be at rest when nobody praises me, and when I am blamed or despised. It is to have a blessed home in the Lord, where I can go in and shut the door, and kneel to my Father in secret, and am at peace as in a deep sea of calmness, when all around and above is trouble.[3]

That's the kind of heart God wants you to have when you come before Him. Prayer is not about you and your wants. It is about spending time in His presence and seeking to do His will.

The bottom line is this: prayer has nothing to do with you. It has everything to do with Jesus. Prayer is about honoring God. Prayer is not about platitudes, but it is all about gratitude. Prayer is not to be focused on *self* but ought to be fixated on the One who is Self-Sufficient.

Consider Jesus for a minute. From start to finish, He lived in constant obedience to the Father (Hebrews 5:8)—even to the point of death (Philippians 2:8). Jesus declared, "My food is to do the will of him who sent me and to accomplish his work" (John 4:34). The night He was betrayed, Jesus confidently prayed, "I've accomplished the work that you gave me to do" (John 17:4). In His final agonizing moments

*Do you have a desire to have deeper conversations with God?*

on the Cross, Jesus pronounced, "Father, into your hands I commit my spirit" (Luke 23:46).

Jesus is truly the ultimate example. His obedience before the Father is what we should strive to emulate on a constant basis.

How would you describe your prayer life? Do you have a desire to have deeper conversations with God? Are you struggling to figure out why your prayers are seemingly not being answered?

Too often our moments with God are interrupted because we let our busy schedules, frustrations, and doubts spoil opportunities to pray. But the more time you spend in God's presence, the better you will understand His will for your life. In Colossians 4:2, Paul writes, "Devote yourselves to prayer, being watchful and thankful." Prayer takes discipline. It takes perseverance and a heart of thankfulness. The more you learn these qualities of prayer, the stronger your prayers will be. Whether you are a novice or a prayer warrior, we encourage you to use Jesus' outline of prayer not only to guide you in your communication with Him but also to help you hear from Him.

To capture the purest form of prayer, look no further than to the "Lord's Prayer" recorded in Matthew 6:9-13. In this passage Jesus teaches how we should pray:

*Our Father in heaven,*
*hallowed be your name,*
*Your kingdom come,*

*your will be done,*
*On earth as it is in heaven.*
*Give us today our daily bread.*
*And forgive us our debts,*
*as we also have forgiven our debtors.*
*And lead us not into temptation,*
*but deliver us from the evil one.*

Notice the unique elements of the prayer Jesus offered. Prayer is about (1) bringing *adoration* (v. 9), (2) yielding *submission* (v. 10), (3) making *petitions* (v. 11), (4) offering *confession* (v. 12), and (5) pursuing *consecration* (v. 13).

According to Jesus, prayer is about praising, honoring, submitting, asking, confessing, and consecrating your life before God. Pray the way God instructs you to pray and be willing to do what He says to do. This may be hard, but it's something you must learn to do in your life. Otherwise, your prayer life will never grow to its fullness.

*Pray the way God instructs you to pray and be willing to do what He says to do.*

## Praying for Your Children

A while back, my wife and I (Jason) were in a prayer group where much time was spent lifting up the marriages and families in our church. After prayer ended, a few of us stayed behind talking. There was one person in particular whose prayers were very deep. We could tell she carried a heartfelt burden for her children, and she displayed a great love and faith in God. So I asked her to share insights on her relentless prayer for her children.

Here's a portion of her message. We hope her honesty will touch you as much as it touched us:

When I would get angry with my prodigal son, I found it extremely difficult to pray for him. I just couldn't find the words. So when I tried to pray for my son, everything I prayed sounded rehearsed and flat. It felt disingenuous. After reading different books on prayer, I found there was no quick solution, no happy ending, no return of the prodigal, no miraculous answers or healing. And then I entered the hardest prayer season of my life. This is a really hard place to land. To give up all control and expectation—and to trust in Jesus completely, and turn my child over to Him. It has been an exhausting and yet beautiful faith journey where He has literally pried my fingers off of my son so that I could release him to Jesus. My prayers today begin much more like, "Lord, whatever it takes . . ." I now pray daily that God will draw near to my son. That he will be reminded of God's precepts that were written on his heart as a youth. I am constantly praying to God that my son will know that he belongs to God and that his identity is in Him. I pray that God sends the hounds of heaven after my son until he repents and submits to God's plan for his life. That my son will seek first the Kingdom of God and not the riches of this world. I pray that my son will stumble on his own path, causing him to be desperate for God. That he would be caught quickly in lies and misconceptions. That he would be a man after God's own heart and that he would grow to love God with all of his heart, mind, and strength. I must admit, it is a humbling experience to parent a prodigal. But it gives you a wonderful insight into the heart of God.

Praying for our children is one of the greatest things we can do for them. It is more important than paying for their college, sending them money, or buying them gifts. Parents, praying for your children is powerful. Your millennial needs your prayers. He or she may not ask you to pray, but your son or daughter desperately needs your prayers.

*Your millennial needs your prayers.*

I (Jason) remember vividly a picture my mom placed on my bedroom bookshelf. It depicted a father kneeling at the bedside of his son. The father's face is buried in his hands, signifying he is interceding for his son. Behind him is an arched window with the splendor of a shining angel. It's a remarkable picture that shows the power of a praying father and the intense warfare that rages over the souls of children. My mom put it in my room to remind me that she and my dad were praying for me.

Several years after my mother's death, I was lying in bed. It was late, but I couldn't sleep. I'd been having nightmares and felt under attack by the evil one. I was scared to tell anyone but shared it with Joe, one of my older brothers, who then shared it with my dad unbeknownst to me. I remember distinctly falling into a deep sleep, and then being awakened by what sounded like whispering prayers. What I didn't realize was those sounds coming up the staircase were the sounds of prayers coming from my dad. He was interceding for me! That morning my dad and I talked about spiritual warfare and why he stayed up praying for me. It changed my outlook on prayer.

*Your prayers are mighty weapons used on behalf of your children to fight off Satan.*

Your prayers matter. Your prayers are mighty weapons used on behalf of your children to fight off Satan. Your prayers have the power to protect your children and provide them with opportunity after opportunity to grow in their relationship with God and with you.

It's disheartening to hear from parents who lack the confidence to pray bold prayers. We know of many, and we identify with those who struggle as well. But we have good news for you: the Bible is filled with many amazing prayers. All you need to do is take some of these prayers recorded in the Bible, learn to follow their patterns, and adapt them as guides for praying for your children.

Here are three types of prayers derived from Scripture to use as prayer maps for praying over your children.[4]

## Pray That Your Millennial Will Walk Worthy of the Gospel

> With this in mind, we constantly pray for you,
> that our God may make you worthy of his calling,
> and that by his power he may bring to fruition
> your every desire for goodness and your every deed
> prompted by faith. We pray this so that the name
> of our Lord Jesus may be glorified in you, and you
> in him, according to the grace of our God and the
> Lord Jesus Christ.
>
> 2 THESSALONIANS 1:11-12

Based on this prayer of Paul to the Thessalonians, pray over your millennial in these three areas:

- Pray that your child will walk worthy of God's calling for his or her life.
- Pray that God's power may be evident in his or her life.
- Pray that God may be glorified in all that your child does.

## Pray That Your Millennial Will Live an Abundant Life

> I give thanks to my God always for you because of
> the grace of God that was given you in Christ Jesus,
> that in every way you were enriched in him in all
> speech and all knowledge—even as the testimony

about Christ was confirmed among you—so that
you are not lacking in any gift, as you wait for the
revealing of our Lord Jesus Christ, who will sustain
you to the end, guiltless in the day of our Lord Jesus
Christ. God is faithful, by whom you were called
into the fellowship of his Son, Jesus Christ our Lord.

1 CORINTHIANS 1:4-9

Based on this prayer of Paul to the Corinthians, pray over
your millennial in these five areas:

- Pray that the grace of God abounds in his or her life.
- Pray that his or her words, thoughts and actions are
  enriched in God's truth.
- Pray that your child doesn't lack anything needed to
  serve God.
- Pray that your son or daughter focus on heavenly
  matters, not just earthly things.
- Pray that your child lives a holy life.

## Pray That Your Millennial Will Please God

And so, from the day we heard, we have not ceased
to pray for you, asking that you may be filled with
the knowledge of his will in all spiritual wisdom and
understanding, so as to walk in a manner worthy of
the Lord, fully pleasing to him, bearing fruit in every
good work and increasing in the knowledge of God.

May you be strengthened with all power, according
to his glorious might, for all endurance and patience
with joy.

COLOSSIANS 1:9-11

Based on this prayer of Paul to the Colossians, pray over your millennial in these five areas:

- Pray that he or she is filled with the knowledge of God.
- Pray that your child knows and pursues God's will for his or her life.
- Pray that your son or daughter grows in wisdom and understanding.
- Pray that your child lives a life of purity and pleases the Lord in all that he or she does.
- Pray that your son or daughter would be strengthened in the Holy Spirit and will experience endurance and joy in his or her life.

Understanding the power of prayer and the impact your prayers can have on your millennial will radically change your life. There aren't many guarantees raising children, but one thing is sure—your prayers can change their lives for the better.

Keep praying, mom and dad. Don't give up! Stay in the fight by staying on your knees.

Chapter 12

# BUILD A FOUNDATION OF BIBLICAL TRUTH

"I don't know what happened to my son."

I (Jason) listened as this dad expressed confusion over whether his son was a Christian. After hearing the dad talk for nearly an hour, I asked one simple question: "Have you ever sat down with your son and asked what he believes and why?"

The dad looked at me blankly. His poor son had been on the receiving end of a one-sided discussion (essentially a continuous lecture) from his dad, without getting to express how he felt. His dad was so busy trying to convince him of the errors of his ways that he forgot to include his son in the conversation.

The dad was pretty upset with himself at this point. So I put my hand on his shoulder and said, "You need to let your son share his heart with you. Otherwise, the only thing you will be reinforcing is that you don't care what he thinks. *Is that what you want?*"

It was as if a lightbulb came on. This father entered my office frustrated and upset, but after deciding to adjust his approach, he left refreshed and ready.

Throughout this book, we've focused on overcoming obstacles and finding ways to engage and bridge the gap with your millennial. We've also been sensitive to the fact that many of you (particularly fathers) weren't as involved as you should have been in the spiritual development of your kids when they were younger. This absence can lead a young person to lack a clear and robust biblical worldview. Take, for example, this conversation I (Jason) had with a mother during a Stand Strong Tour in Texas.

Alex and I had a great weekend challenging young people in the truth and relevance of God's Word. We laid out a strong case for the reliability of the Bible—the overwhelming evidence for the resurrection—and the sovereign power and control of God. We felt God moving in a powerful way.

As I packed my stuff, a mother approached with tears running down her face. We sat together, and I asked about her grief. Struggling to control her emotions, she described her son and his issues: "I just hurt so much for my son. He says he wants to live for God, but he won't give up porn and smoking marijuana."

My heart broke for this mom. My heart also broke for her son.

As she shared her struggles and fears about her son, she began receiving texts from him. She showed me his response to her texted question: *Do you love your sin more than God?* He replied: *Not happy about how I'm living but don't think God is the answer.*

This mother confessed that she and her husband weren't the best examples to their kids. Earlier in their marriage, they had separated. Her husband liked to hang with the boys and drink. They said they were a Christian family, but they didn't really model it or equip their kids with a biblical worldview.

## Your Biblical Mandate

As we come to an end to *Abandoned Faith*, it is essential that we examine your personal biblical worldview. We've seen that young people without a robust biblical worldview usually lack parents who model a biblical worldview. Dr. Christian Smith writes, "Most teenagers and their parents may not realize it, but a lot of research in the sociology of religion suggests that the most important social influence in shaping young people's religious lives is the religious life modeled and taught to them by their parents."[1]

So if we expect to see young people develop a biblical worldview, then parents need to start developing a strong biblical worldview. But before we examine your biblical worldview, let's turn to the Bible and see what God's Word mandates for parents.

## The Four Mandates of Parenting

When you were growing up, who did you consider to be the wisest people in your life? Was it your parents? Grandparents? An aunt? Uncle? Maybe a teacher or a friend? God has placed wise people in all of our lives. But the most important people are parents.

**Parents are to bring up their children with godly instruction.**

Parents are to bring up their children with godly instruction. They are to give them insight and instruction on how they ought to live. Solomon told his children, "Hear, O sons, a father's instruction [discipline], and be attentive, that you may gain insight [understanding], for I give you good precepts [doctrine]; do not forsake my teaching [direction, law, instruction]" (Proverbs 4:1-2).

According to Solomon , a parent's job is to discipline, offer understanding, provide solid doctrine, and teach their children the ways of the Lord. Just read these powerful Proverbs that speak to each area of parental responsibility.

*Discipline:* a chastening based on morals; correction that comes with warning, rebuking, and training.

- For the commandment is a lamp and the teaching a light, and the reproofs of discipline are the way of life. (Proverbs 6:23)
- Whoever loves discipline loves knowledge, but he who hates reproof is stupid. (Proverbs 12:1)

- Whoever spares the rod hates his son, but he who loves him is diligent to discipline him. (Proverbs 13:24)

*Insight/Understanding:* the power to see into a situation and gain the insight to know what to do.

- Get wisdom; get insight; do not forget, and do not turn away from the words of my mouth. (Proverbs 4:5)
- Say to wisdom, "You are my sister," and call insight your intimate friend. (Proverbs 7:4)
- Leave your simple ways, and live, and walk in the way of insight. (Proverbs 9:6)

*Precepts/Doctrine/Law:* to grasp and learn teachings that you have come to believe are true.

- For I give you good precepts; do not forsake my teaching. (Proverbs 4:2)
- If one turns away his ear from hearing the law, even his prayer is an abomination. (Proverbs 28:9)
- The one who keeps the law is a son with understanding, but a companion of gluttons shames his father. (Proverbs 28:7)

*Teaching/Instruction:* to guide and offer counsel and direction.

- Hear, my son, your father's instruction, and forsake not your mother's teaching. (Proverbs 1:8)

- My son, do not forget my teaching, but let your heart keep my commandments. (Proverbs 3:1)
- Keep my commandments and live; keep my teaching as the apple of your eye. (Proverbs 7:2)
- The teaching of the wise is a fountain of life, that one may turn away from the snares of death. (Proverbs 13:14)

It's not enough to just provide materially for our children. It's the sole duty and highest responsibility for parents to cultivate spiritual truths in their children's lives as well. How this plays out in your life depends on your relationship with your millennial and whether he or she has a relationship with God. These relational factors will determine what you can and can't do. It's like doing gymnastics: you're going to have to be very flexible just to keep the relationship intact. So get stretching!

*You're going to have to be very flexible just to keep the relationship intact.*

No matter the hardship, remember that you are not alone. There have been and still remain millions of godly parents who have been wonderful spiritual mentors to their adult children. We believe you can be one too!

Jim Daly, president of Focus on the Family, offers this wise counsel for parents:

The Bible charges parents with certain objectives, and these don't change just because your child grows up: we are to help our children become followers of

Christ, godly men and women (Malachi 2:15 and Ephesians 6:4). Parents of adult children would be wise, then, to view their decision-making with this ultimate goal in mind. Doing this will provide clarity of thought and insight into when to provide "tough love," when to speak or remain silent, or when to lend a helping hand or not. Measure your child's actions against the fruit of the Spirit. Ask yourself how your child is becoming equipped to one day become a husband or a wife, a father or a mother. Consider how what you do or say will impact your child's walk with the Lord.[2]

Seek God and your spouse for clarity of thought as you exercise and fulfill your biblical mandates as a parent: to discipline, give insight to, guide, and instruct your children in the truth of God's Word. So as you work to be that spiritual mentor in your millennial's life, never let Satan, or anyone for that matter, convince you that your role no longer matters. It does and always will matter.

## Examine Your Faith

D. L. Moody said, "A man ought to live so that everybody knows he is a Christian . . . and most of all, his family ought to know." What a powerful yet convicting statement. According to Moody, parents are to work hard at being the best models of Christianity for their children. But to be the best model, parents must be willing to do a self-inventory on their beliefs as Christians. Paul stated, "Examine yourselves to see whether you are in the faith. Test yourselves. Or do you not realize this about yourselves, that Jesus Christ is in you?—unless indeed you fail to meet the test!" (2 Corinthians 13:5).

*Parents must be willing to do a self-inventory on their beliefs as Christians.*

Some parents have failed to personally and holistically raise their children with a biblical worldview. Bible illiteracy among Christians has resulted in widespread confusion among millennials about Christianity. Too many millennials are also unable to think critically. As a result, they have a framework of Christianity that, quite frankly, is not rooted in Christianity at all.

For instance, some Christian millennials measure and interpret their faith in four ways:

1. They *perform* certain good works that align with what they believe to be morally right.
2. They avoid certain bad habits to look as though they are growing in their faith.
3. They act a certain way to gain acceptance from others.
4. They classify their faith as a self-indulgent behavior that works for them.

A trace of this bad theology often stems from one or both parents. At some point in a child's life, any one of these incorrect views was either taught or caught in the home.

That's why when we teach parental courses, we help parents regroup by reexamining their faith. We help them get to a place of confidence in what they believe. We tell parents their faith must be tried and tested. Not only does their faith need strong theological backing, it needs to be personal and communal as well.

*We tell parents their faith must be tried and tested.*

We are seeing thousands of parents at our Stand Strong Tours and Truth for a New Generation apologetic conferences. We receive tons of positive feedback after they read our biblical worldview books. It's really exciting. But it is also a reminder that we have a long road ahead. There are millions of parents who raised their children without a robust biblical worldview. Now that they've seen the damage it has done, they are crying out for answers.

When a parent shows signs of continual spiritual growth, it encourages his or her millennial to do likewise, and it can have a real positive impact. We're not saying the millennial child will convert or return to Christ—but a parent's example will definitely make an impression. Your effort to grow spiritually conveys to your millennial that you are hungry to learn, though you don't have all the answers. You don't have everything together, but you are still allowing God to teach (or perhaps re-teach) you. Spiritual growth communicates that faith is more than something you believe in—it defines who you are. Sean McDowell puts it like this: "Relationships engender our beliefs. Beliefs then contribute to the formation of our values, which in turn drive our behavior."[3]

As believers in Christ, we should never be satisfied with our current status in our walk with Christ. We should always strive to know Him more. To love Him more. To tell more people about the gospel of Jesus Christ. We should always be searching the Scriptures to learn new things, be convicted in His Word, and share with others what the Bible says.

*As you work through this process, please don't do it alone.*

As you work through this process, please don't do it alone. The wife is not to do everything and the husband to do nothing. That's part of the problem in many "Christian" homes. When problems escalate with the kids, dad is too insecure, embarrassed, or frustrated to deal with them. We can't tell you how many conversations we have had with parents in the church that fit this description.

I (Jason) want to share a letter I received from a hurting mother. To add some context, the mother is distraught over the fact that her son got engaged to a woman who is not a Christian. Here's what she wrote:

After hearing [that] my son proposed to his girlfriend, I wasn't supportive of it, but responded vaguely because I didn't want to condemn it outright to his face. As usual, my husband had nothing to say. The leadership role in our home is continually dropped because of low spiritual priorities. I guess my husband is just trying to keep his own head above water, plus he can't seem to do the hard things with our adult children, especially in the area of spirituality. My husband thinks there is nothing wrong with this picture, and yet my heart is grieved over this. Honestly, I could beat myself up day and night, and feel totally hopeless and guilty for all the decisions I've made that have helped land us here. But because I belong to God, I choose to turn my face toward the Lord and keep steadily looking to Him for hope, peace, wisdom, guidance and joy. I praise Him for getting my broken family this far! It has been totally God! I believe He still does miracles, and [I'm] praying He will do a big miracle in my family.

It's heartbreaking to receive letters, messages, and emails like this from parents. But it's letters like this that remind us to pray—to take comfort that when Jesus left, He sent us the greatest Comforter, the Holy Spirit. He is using all of us to bear one another's burdens and lift each other up in the love of Christ.

*In the midst of great suffering, we need to band together*

So if you are stuck in a rut with your millennial or spouse, please don't remain there alone. Get the help you need. It might bruise your ego, but do it, because it's the right thing to do. In the midst of great suffering, we need to band together, which is why we so desperately want to work with churches to help unite families and bring family members back to God.

## Know the Fundamentals

We've walked through biblical mandates for parents and covered challenges in modeling Christ to your millennial. Now we turn our attention to some of the major tenets of the Christian faith. Though we are apologists and theologians, limited space in this book won't allow us to fully articulate and expound upon the beliefs of Christianity. To grow in your understanding and defense of the Christian faith, please check out our ministry websites, standstrongministries.org and alexmcfarland.com for helpful resources.

The following abridged list contains fundamentals that every follower of Christ ought to know, live, and defend.

### The Bible

The Holy Bible contains 66 books that have been inspired by God to be true and authentic. It is divided into two sections: Old and New Testaments (Covenants). The Bible contains the substance of answers when dealing with God's truth, holy living, life issues and situations, wisdom, counsel, rewards, justice, and the glory of God (2 Timothy 3:15-16).

### God

God transcends space, time, and matter. Yet we know Him because He has revealed himself to us. The Bible says, "Long ago, at many times and in many ways, God spoke to our fathers by the prophets, but in these last days he has spoken to us by his Son, whom he appointed the heir of all things, through whom also he created the world" (Hebrews 1:1-2).

Christians believe in the unity, simplicity, and tri-unity of God. We believe there are not many gods, but one God (unity). We believe that God is not a composed Being made up of parts but that He is indivisible and undivided (simplicity). And finally, we believe God is a plurality of persons (Father, Son, and Holy Spirit) within the unity of the Godhead (tri-unity). Regarding the attributes (character) of God, Paul Little writes, "All the attributes of God are in perfect harmony and are in no way antagonistic to each other. God's love and mercy are not opposed to, or exercised at the expense of, His righteousness and holiness."[4]

## Jesus Christ

In Matthew 16:15, Jesus asked Peter, "Who do you say that I am?" The bottom line is Jesus is fully God (Titus 2:13) and fully man (Hebrews 2:16-18). To deny or cheapen any of the two natures in the Person of Christ is to possess a false and unbiblical view of Him. Jesus is our Savior (Matthew 1:21; John 1:29, 33) who paid the penalty of our sins on the Cross, but defeated sin and death by rising from the dead (1 Corinthians 15:4). Paul writes, "Though he [Jesus] was rich, yet for your sake he became poor, so that you by his poverty might become rich" (2 Corinthians 8:9).

## Christ's Death

Christianity is established on the historical *fact* that Christ died on the Cross for our sins approximately 2,000 years ago. It is clear, according to Scripture, that Christ's death was prophesied beforehand (Isaiah 52:13–53:12). Furthermore, Christ himself predicted His unique death on the Cross (John 2:19-22). Christ's death on the Cross was atonement for our sins (2 Corinthians 5:14-15). Salvation would not be possible had Christ not offered His life in exchange for our sins. It is by and through the death and resurrection of Jesus Christ that we are given victory over sin (1 Corinthians 15:57).

## Man and Sin

The Bible teaches, "All have sinned and fall short of the glory of God" (Romans 3:23). This is known as the doctrine of original sin. Sin came into the world by free will. Man *freely* choose to disobey God, and therefore sinned against Him (Romans 3:10-18).

## The Holy Spirit

The Holy Spirit is the third person of the Triune Godhead (1 Corinthians 2:11; Ephesians 4:4). The Bible teaches several pivotal roles and qualities of the Holy Spirit. He has emotions (Ephesians 4:30). He has a sovereign will (1 Corinthians 12:11; James 1:18). He gives life (Romans 8:2). He is eternal (Hebrews 9:14). He is omnipotent (Job 33:4). He is omniscient (1 Corinthians 2:10-12; Romans 11:33). He is also omnipresent (John 14:17). The work of the Holy Spirit is to convict the world of sin, righteousness, and judgment (John 16:7-11). It is the Holy Spirit who inspired the Scriptures (2 Peter 1:21), regenerates the sinner (Titus 3:5), and makes intercession for us (Romans 8:26).

## The Church

The Greek word for church in the New Testament is *ekklesia*. It means "called out." The church is an assembly of believers (Ephesians 4:12); who meet regularly (Hebrews 10:25) as one body (1 Corinthians 12:13); edify one another (Ephesians 4:12); and worship Jesus, who is the Head of the church (Ephesians 1:21).

## Salvation

Jonah declared, "Salvation belongs to the Lord" (Jonah 2:9). Paul writes, "For by grace you have been saved through faith. And this is not your own doing; it is the gift of God, not a result of works, so that no one may boast" (Ephesians 2:8-9). Thus, salvation is a free gift to anyone who believes (John 1:12; John 3:16; Romans 5:18).

## Second Coming

Jesus Christ came into this world at a historical point in time as a baby (Luke 2). Likewise, Jesus Christ will return a second time. Yet this time, He will come as King (Zechariah 14:9) to establish His Kingdom on earth (Revelation 20:1-7). All the people who rejected Christ as their Savior will appear before The Great White Throne Judgment and receive their final destruction forever (Revelation 20:11-15). Jesus Christ will then usher in the New Heaven and New Earth (Revelation 21–22), where there will be no more sin, only the eternal love and reign of God.

## Are You Sure?

Think back to the time your son or daughter came to Christ. What do you remember? Obviously, if your child never did receive the gift of salvation, then you can't. But if you believe he or she did, what stands out to you?

*One major reason Christianity is declining is that initial conversions were not true conversions.*

In this book, we have examined the major decline of Christianity among young people. One major reason Christianity is declining is that *initial* conversions were not *true* conversions. So it's important to understand your child's conversion experience and whether your son or daughter actually did accept Christ as Lord and Savior.

I (Jason) remember a couple who came to see me in my office. They had been struggling for years with their son's actions. He never seemed to listen and was engaged in promiscuous behavior. These parents explained that they often reminded their son about the truth of God's Word and his need to stop sinning. But he never would. At one point, the dad said he wasn't even sure his son was a Christian. The mom jumped on him for that.

I quickly came to his rescue by asking a legitimate question: "But is he *really*?" The mom insisted her son was a Christian because she led him to the Lord when he was seven years old.

I asked many more questions: "What prompted your son

to ask Jesus to come into his life? How did you share the gospel with him? Did he comprehend it completely and fully for himself? What was your son's life like before and after? If he is truly a Christian, why doesn't he feel convicted by his sin? If he is truly a Christian, why doesn't he ever read the Bible and desire to use his spiritual gifts? If he is truly a Christian, why doesn't he have any Christian friends?"

You might be thinking, *You were grilling those poor folks!*

At the end of my "interrogation," the parents realized that all they could base their son's conversion on was a little prayer he repeated. The mom turned to her husband and said, "This whole time I believed our son was saved because he prayed a prayer I told him to pray. But now that I look back, it was something he did because he knew I wanted him to do it."

The dad looked up sheepishly to say, "That's what he's been telling us, honey. Every time he feels judged by us, he tells us that he doesn't believe what we believe. But you keep telling him that he accepted Christ when he was a child."

The meeting was definitely an eye-opener for all of us. As they were leaving, I offered to meet with their son. They weren't sure he'd agree to meet. So we prayed and asked the Lord to set it up. The following week, their son was in my office.

At this point, I knew this young college student wasn't a Christian. So that's how I started the conversation. He was a bit surprised but relieved. I told him I didn't want him to feel cornered, judged, or pressured to feel or think a certain way—but just to be himself. We spent a few hours asking each other a million questions. At the end of our time he knew that he was a sinner and that Jesus died and rose again so that he could have eternal life. I joined him as he openly confessed with his mouth that Jesus is Lord and Savior of his life.

When the news reached his parents, they were beside themselves. They now could expect their son's actions to grow out of a real relationship with Jesus. It would make all the difference in their future communication.

## A True Shepherd's Love

First Thessalonians 2:3-20 is one of the richest and most intimate expressions of Paul in all his epistles. Open up your Bible and read it. Here we see the love of a true shepherd. Paul loved the people he was called to minister to so much that he referred to them as his children. He didn't just encourage them and tell them to be more like Jesus. He likened his love for the Thessalonians to that of a nursing mother and protective father. What love Paul had for the church!

*We know this is the kind of love you have for your millennial.*

We know this is the kind of love you have for your millennial. Given all the dilemmas parents face and the difficult questions that pile up each day, we wanted to summarize (and apply to parenting) 1 Thessalonians 2 to embolden you to keep reinforcing biblical truth in your child's life.

Life Lessons from the Apostle Paul

1. Be careful that your parenting is not deceptive (v. 3).
2. Be faithful in your stewardship as a parent. You have been entrusted as a parent and are called to preach the gospel to your family (v. 4).
3. Be sincere in your contentment. Make sure you don't choose money or fame over your family (v. 5).
4. Be humble. Don't allow the praise of man to compromise your relationship with God and your family (v. 6).
5. Be gentle and patient in understanding. Seek opportunities to immerse your millennial in the teachings of Jesus (v. 7).
6. Be affectionate and willing to make sacrifices for your family (v. 8).
7. Be a good example of a hard worker who isn't a burden to anyone (v. 9).
8. Be blameless in your family (v. 10).
9. Be consistent in encouraging, comforting, and exhorting your millennial to live worthy of God, not you (vv. 11-12).

A man who we believe exemplifies the life lessons of 1 Thessalonians 2 is one many Christians know. Many consider him to be one of the greatest defenders of the faith. His name is Lee Strobel. If you have never heard his testimony, please do a YouTube search and watch Lee share his story.

Much can be said about his impressive career as a journalist, writer, speaker, and defender of the faith. But what we are especially impressed with is how much Lee loves, adores, and invests in his children and grandchildren.

*"How do you help millennials who carry a lot of doubt about the Bible and Jesus?"*

Through the years, we have had the joy of spending time with Lee. He has challenged and encouraged us tremendously.

So while writing this book, we asked Lee for some parenting perspectives. Specifically, we asked: "How do you help millennials who carry a lot of doubt about the Bible and Jesus?"

Lee's response was marked with wisdom, yet also came with a challenge for all to hear:

> I really think that our young people aren't looking for froth or entertainment. They want substance. They want to deal with these issues and find the answers to their spiritual questions. I believe this is a wide-open door to apologetics, which essentially is evangelism. And that gives me hope, because when we engage young people by reducing their questions down, we are able to then address each one in a meaningful way. And this shouldn't intimidate us because we have good answers to the toughest questions about faith and life. So when millennials get to the point where they are honestly wrestling with these things, I think that's wonderful—because

if they come with an open heart and mind, they will emerge with a stronger faith. But older Christians, particularly parents, need to be ready to have answers and engage young people with a strong understanding of the Christian faith. Otherwise, they won't have the adequate answers young people are seeking.

So mom and dad, in what ways are you reducing your millennial's spiritual questions and addressing them in a way that speaks to them? Through the years, how fruitful have your answers been to your millennial's questions about God, the Bible, salvation, and cultural and ethical issues? Whatever your track record has been, it's never too late to be that example and voice of biblical reason. God has called you to reinforce biblical truth in the lives of your children. So get to it!

# JESUS IS THE KEY

PEOPLE EVERYWHERE invest their lives in the search for meaning, purpose, and fulfillment. They seek something more than money, fame, luxurious houses, good looks, nice cars, or a lucrative stock portfolio. Nothing is wrong with these things, but they cannot provide peace to the soul or forgiveness of one's sin.

Did you know that the highest rates of suicide and divorce occur among the most affluent classes of society? On the West Coast, psychologists and counselors have isolated a new affliction and given it a name: "Sudden Acquired Wealth Syndrome." People are achieving every benchmark that our society says should make them happy, but they are

*People today truly are looking for meaningful answers, craving hope in a dangerous world.*

finding it's possible to be materially rich yet spiritually bankrupt. Many have schedules that are full but hearts that are empty.

Several years ago, our nine-member ministry team crossed America on a 50-states-in-50-days trip. During the course of this journey, I (Alex) preached in every service, in all 50 US states, and personally spoke with thousands of people. We had the privilege of hosting 64 worship services throughout the entire country. Our outreach team met people with probing questions and genuine concern about spiritual issues. People today truly are looking for meaningful answers, craving hope in a dangerous world.

Present realities such as worldwide terrorist attacks, global economic uncertainty, political instability, and natural disasters such as Hurricane Katrina have only intensified this search.

Immediately after the terrorist attacks of 9/11, I went to New York City to help with a prayer center that had been set up by the Billy Graham ministry and Samaritan's Purse. As I had on the 50-state tour, I spoke daily to hundreds of people from every background imaginable. They may have expressed themselves in different ways, but they all had the same basic question: "Who is God, and how may I come to know Him?"

Where one stands with God is the most vital of all issues, but the good news is that you may settle this today! You may have wondered, "How does a person become a Christian? How can I be certain that my sin is forgiven? How may I experience consistent spiritual growth?" Let's consider these things together.

## God's Word Explains the Message of Salvation

Jesus said in John 3:3, "Unless one man is born again he cannot see the kingdom of God." Salvation is the issue. The most important question you will ever ask yourself is this: *Do I know for certain that I have eternal life, and that I will go to heaven when I die?*

If you stood before God right now and God asked, "Why should I let you into my heaven?", what would you say?

The Bible describes our condition: "For all have sinned and fall short of the glory of God" (Romans 3:23). Just as a job pays a wage at the end of the week, our sins will yield a result at the end of a lifetime. "For the wages of sin is death [the Bible describes this as separation from God, the punishment of hell], but the free gift of God is eternal life in Christ Jesus our Lord" (Romans 6:23).

*God's love for you is shown by His provision for your need.*

God's love for you is shown by His provision for your need: "But God shows his love for us in that while we were still sinners, Christ died for us" (Romans 5:8).

Salvation requires repentance, which means a "turning." Jesus said, "Unless you repent, you will all likewise perish" (Luke 13:3). The New Testament emphasizes the necessity of repentance and salvation: "Repent therefore, and turn back, that your sins may be blotted out" (Acts 3:19).

Every one of us has sinned, and the Bible says that our sins must be dealt with. We have a two-fold sin problem. We are sinners by birth, and we are sinners by choice.

Someone once said to the great evangelist Dr. Vance Havner, "This thing about man's sin nature, I find that hard to swallow!" Dr. Havner answered, "You don't have to swallow it—you're born with it, it's already in you."

The world classifies sin, viewing some sins as worse than others. But the Bible teaches that all sin is an offense against God, and even one sin is serious enough to keep a person out of heaven. You may not have robbed a bank—or maybe you have. God doesn't grade on a curve; humanity is a tainted race, and sin is the problem.

Often in life, we know what is right, but we do what is wrong. You may have even looked back and wondered, "What was I thinking? Why did I do that? How could I have said that?" Jesus said that man needs to repent and make a change. Repentance means turning *from* your sins and *to* Christ. By faith, trust *who* Jesus is (God's Son, mankind's Savior) and *what* Jesus did (died in your place and rose from the dead).

God's forgiveness is received by faith. We are to confess our faith before others, unashamed to let the world know that we believe in Jesus: "If you confess with your mouth that Jesus is Lord and believe in your heart that God raised him from the dead, you will be saved. For with the heart one believes and is justified, and with the mouth one confesses and is saved" (Romans 10:9-10).

What is faith? Faith is trust. It is simple, honest, childlike trust. God says that you have a sin problem, *Do you trust* but He loves you and will forgive you. God *what God has* says that through Jesus Christ, He has made *said and what* a way for anyone to be saved who will come *God has done?* to Him. Do you trust what God has said and what God has done? If you come to Christ in belief and faith, God promises to save you: "For everyone who calls on the name of the Lord will be saved" (Romans 10:13). Jesus promises, "Whoever comes to me I will never cast out" (John 6:37).

If you desire to have a relationship with the Lord, that can be accomplished right where you are now. Make your journey to the Cross today, through this basic prayer of commitment:

Dear Lord Jesus, I know that I have sinned, and I cannot save myself. I believe that you are the Son of God, and that you died and rose again for me, to forgive my sins and to be my Savior. I turn from my sins, and I ask you to forgive me. I receive you into my life as my Lord and Savior. Jesus, thank You for saving me now. Help me to live the rest of my life for You. Amen.

## God's Word Gives You Assurance of Salvation

You can overcome doubts about where you stand with God. Based on what God's Word says (not what you feel or assume), you can know that you have eternal life: "Whoever has the Son has life; whoever does not have the Son of God does not have life. I write these things to you who believe in the name of the Son of God that you may

**Your merit before God is totally based on Jesus.**

know that you have eternal life" (1 John 5:12-13).

Jesus said, "Whoever hears my word and believes him who sent me has eternal life. He does not come into judgment, but has passed from death unto life" (John 5:24). Remember: You are not saved by good works, and you are not "kept saved" by good works. Your merit before God is totally based on Jesus. His perfection, holiness, and righteousness is credited to each one who believes in God's Word and His promises.

## What Is Meant by the Term "Rededication"?

A news reporter once asked me (Alex) this question. He heard me use this term as I spoke at a church, and he wanted to know what I meant. "Rededication" is for a believer who desires his or her walk with Christ to be renewed and deepened. A Christian can wander from God in sin or simply lose true closeness with the Lord through the busyness of life.

A born-again Christian is forever God's child. Your salvation is a matter of *sonship*. Your daily Christian growth is a matter of *fellowship*. Your spiritual birth into God's family is in some ways similar to your physical birth into the human family. For instance, when growing up, you may have disobeyed and disappointed your father. Something you did may have grieved your father, but you were still his child.

In the same way, our Christian relationship with the Lord is still intact, even though a sin we commit may hinder our daily fellowship with God. Salvation is a one-time, instantaneous event; Christian growth and personal fellowship with God is an everyday, lifelong process. Consistent daily prayer, Bible study, obedience to the Holy Spirit, and church fellowship are all keys to growth and Christian maturity.

*God lovingly receives all who turn to Him, and all who return to Him!*

God lovingly receives all who *turn* to Him and all who *return* to Him! He cleanses us from sin and restores us to fellowship with Him. King David had been "a man after God's own heart," but his sinful deeds required that he humbly recommit himself to the Lord: "Cast me not away from your presence. . . . Restore to me the joy of your salvation" (Psalms 51:11-12). Christian publications often use the following verse in the context of evangelism, and that's okay; but 1 John 1:9 is really a promise to the Christian who needs to make things right with the Lord: "If we confess our sins, he is faithful and just to forgive us our sins and to cleanse us from all unrighteousness."

You may already know the Lord but wish to pray these basic words of rededication and commitment:

Lord Jesus, I acknowledge that I have sinned and wandered from You. I confess my sin and turn from it. I recommit myself to You as Lord. Thank You for forgiving me; I trust You to give me the strength to live for You each day of my life. Thank You for being my Savior, my Lord, and my friend. Amen.

May God bless you as you journey on with Him.

# WHEN THERE IS A FAILURE TO LAUNCH

INDEPENDENT LIVING FOR your adult child is a journey, not a destination. It may not happen in one day, but it needs to happen someday. It is your responsibility as a parent to help guide your child toward this goal. The following steps can help encourage a reasonable solution for your adult child, one that's best for all involved.

*First, establish a timeline.* Do you know when your adult child plans to move out? If you don't have a deadline yet, this is where to begin. This conversation will be a difficult one, so expect resistance. However, it is important to take the initiative to bring up the question of *when*.

The best-case scenario is to allow your adult child to suggest a move-out date. For example, if your child is serious, he or she may say, "My goal is to move out by October so I can be in a place before my next birthday." If this is true, both of you can agree to an October 31 deadline and move forward accordingly. It's much better to help achieve a move-out date than to invest in a seemingly endless process of feeding and caring for your adult child.

But what if your adult child is reluctant to talk about when to move out? If this is the case, you are left with the difficult decision of creating a timeline. Be clear with your son or daughter. You may even want to put an agreement in writing, with both of you signing a document that says your child will move out by a specific date.

Once the clock is ticking, it can feel like a season of the television series *24*. You hear the sound of the clock in the background, relentlessly counting down to the last second. When everyone agrees to the goal, the only thing left is to work together to make the goal a reality.

If you're having trouble bringing up the topic of a move, you may need to ask yourself the following questions:

- Are you in a place where your boundaries are being crossed and you need to establish some limits?
- Are you willing to allow your adult child to live in your home within those limits as he or she moves toward independence?
- Does your adult child *want* to become independent, or is he or she comfortable allowing you to take care of all responsibilities?
- Has the situation become so intolerable—perhaps even volatile—that your main concern is getting your adult child out of your house, as quickly and safely as possible?[1]

Assess your situation. When you move beyond emotions and clearly look at the matter, you're likely to establish a reasonable amount of time for you and your child to work together toward independent living. In most cases, 12 months should be the maximum time allowed. Otherwise, the timeline doesn't feel real, and serious effort is unlikely to take place to change the situation. Any amount of time between six and 12 months should be enough to set up a new housing situation and achieve the corresponding income necessary to sustain it.

What if your adult child is not working? Then make this one of the goals in the process. Instead of hanging out with friends or online, your adult child should invest at least eight hours a day, five days a week, into a job search. Anyone who invests this amount of time and effort into finding a job will find something acceptable, leading to positive encouragement to take the next step of independent living.

*Second, view your adult child as a temporary guest instead of a resident.* Once you've determined a time frame for moving out, you can start viewing your adult child as a guest visiting for a period of time instead of a kid living at home indefinitely. Yes, you may offer free meals and hospitality—but not forever. There will be a checkout date by which your child and his or her belongings will have a new location.

This may sound harsh to some, but this mental change can offer a new hope for both you and your adult child. He or she may live at home at the moment, but your child is not a resident of your home. In fact, you can agree that your adult child will pay a certain amount of rent each month, increasing it monthly until the move-out date. This added incentive will further motivate your child to search for housing and realize that time living at home with mom and dad is limited.

*Third, develop clear boundaries.* Your home is yours. You choose the rules. If you choose certain quiet hours, limit guests, or ban alcohol or smoking, you are free to do so. Your child may argue, "I'm an adult! You can't tell me what to do." As long as he or she is living in your home, you get to make the rules. If your child doesn't like the rules, he or she can participate in banned activities elsewhere or find another place to live.

It is important not to make living at home too convenient. You do not need to cook every meal, fold laundry, and do dishes for your son or daughter. If you don't want to pay for a cell phone or provide free wifi, then don't. When real life becomes more "real" at home, adult children will look for another place where they can live as they choose.

*Fourth, cut off the cash.* Are you still giving your son or daughter an allowance? Do you allow your child to have a debit or credit card with access to your accounts? You are not helping your child when you offer free money; you are enabling him or her.

When you cut off the cash to your child, reality quickly hits home. All of the "little" expenses mom and dad have carried for years add up quickly when there is no credit card or cash supplement. End the cash flow, and you may find a quick solution to your child's job search, move from home, or return to college.

*Fifth, create separation at home.* If possible, find ways to make living at home a separate space for your child. For example, if your daughter or son lives in a garage apartment, you can cut off phone, cable, and Internet to the location so he or she will have to go without or purchase services from personal funds. When everything is free, there is little incentive to help. When some services come with conditions, suddenly home is not as comfortable and other options begin to look more appealing.

*Sixth, bring in reinforcements.* You may be tempted to quickly end these "tough love" actions when your child gets into a bind. Don't try to handle this alone. You may need to work in partnership with your spouse, friend, counselor, pastor, or other trusted advisor for encouragement and accountability in those vulnerable moments when you reach your breaking point.

Whether your launch plan takes six weeks, six months, or six years, do your best to make moving day a genuine time of celebration. We're not talking about celebrating that your child is leaving! This is a time to celebrate your child's new place and a new milestone in life. You both have worked long and hard to reach this day. Take time to encourage your son or daughter with words of hope and a party together.

When some adult children leave home, they are uncertain about what their parents might think. *Is Mom happy? Does Dad hate me? Are they glad to get rid of me?* Affirm your love for your child and make plans to continue a close relationship even after the move. Your attitude during this final stage can have a major impact on your relationship in the years that follow.

## How *Not* to Get Your Adult Child to Move Out

Unfortunately, some parents grow frustrated to the point of taking drastic measures. We've heard some funny and not-so-funny stories and share them here to help you understand how *not* to get your adult child to move out.

Do not stealthily place suitcases or moving boxes in your child's room. Some young adults come home at the end of the day to find unexpected moving boxes. The parents think it's funny, but the message is unclear or hurtful to your child. Your child may really want to move out and needs encouragement to do so, not "subtle" hints that confuse and cause anger.

Do not suddenly remodel your adult child's room. One friend returned home from college break as a freshman and found his bedroom had been turned into a hobby room for his dad. The message was clear without saying a word: "Your room is gone, and you are no longer welcome to live here." The lack of communication can be so abrupt and painful that relationships are seriously broken between parent and child.

Do not leave apartment listing guides on your child's bed. You may think this is a funny or subtle way to point your child toward a new home. Your child may interpret it as

"Get out of my house now!" Dropping materials without grace-filled communication may result in real pain and misunderstanding. At least attach a note that says something like "I found a place I thought you might like. Let's visit it Saturday and check it out."

Do not leave your child's belongings on the front porch. Some parents have seriously resorted to this strategy. If your relationship with your child has deteriorated to this point, please seek outside help. It's better to meet with a pastor or counselor to agree on a plan for your child to move out than to simply throw their stuff out like an unwanted guest's. Your child may move, but your relationship may be harmed for years to come.

## Moving Forward in Faith

Your adult child needs to eventually fly away from the nest. You can help or hurt the process through your actions during this time. Some parents look back at these years with warm memories of the best times they've had with their children Others look back with regret over words said and actions taken.

Pray, work together, and seek a path that ends with celebrating the independence of your child in achieving work with meaning and building a life of significance.

# ACKNOWLEDGMENTS

A WORK OF THIS SCOPE would not be possible without the cooperation and investment of many people. Space does not permit naming all of the dedicated individuals who graciously came around this project, but I especially want to thank Larry Weeden and Liz Duckworth of Focus on the Family; the phenomenal team at Tyndale House Publishers; Dr. Tony Beam and Robin McCarter, my valued colleagues at North Greenville University; and especially the dozens of parents, pastors, and Christian leaders who gave of their time to be interviewed for this book. We all share a passion to solidly pass the Christian faith on to those around us.

Thanks are also due to my coauthor and frequent traveling and preaching partner, Reverend Jason Jimenez. Most of all, I thank the Lord Jesus Christ, who is truth, for this and every generation.

*Alex McFarland*

I would like to thank my dad (Phil, aka "Poppie") and my second-mom (Barb, aka "Woo Woo Grammie") for being such awesome parents to me. Dad, thank you for always being there for me and believing in God's call in my life. Mom, thank you for always praying for me and offering words of encouragement. Your love and unyielding support has meant more to me than you two will ever know.

I would also like to express my deepest love and appreciation to my first mother, Amy. Although she passed away when I was only fifteen years old, in those short years my mother taught me what a Christian looks like. Her life and death has had the greatest impact on my life, and I look forward to that day when I will see her in heaven.

Last, I want to thank my good buddy, Jeff Myers, as well as the staff at Summit Ministries. I can't think of a more effective ministry impacting students than Summit. I have been so honored to partner with them, and I am thankful for the small role I get to play each summer, as we disciple students and equip each one of them with an unshakable biblical worldview.

*Jason Jimenez*

# NOTES

## INTRODUCTION: FROM CHRISTIANITY TO ATHEISM

1. Woodrow Kroll, "The New America and the New Bible Illiteracy," *Free Republic*, June 27, 2007, http://freerepublic.com/focus/f-religion/1857058/posts.
2. Cited in "America's Changing Religious Landscape," *Pew Research Center*, May 12, 2015, http://www.pewforum.org/2015/05/12/americas-changing-religious-landscape.
3. David Kinnaman and Gabe Lyons, *UnChristian* (Grand Rapids, MI: Baker Books, 2012), 11.
4. Cited in "Millennials: Confident. Connected. Open to Change," *Pew Research Center*, February 24, 2010, http://www.pewsocialtrends.org/2010/02/24/millennials-confident-connected-open-to-change/.

## CHAPTER ONE: HOPE FOR HURTING PARENTS

1. Mary E. DeMuth, *Building the Christian Family You Never Had: A Practical Guide for Pioneer Parents* (Colorado Springs: WaterBrook, 2006), 122.
2. Bottke, Allison. "When Helping Hurts: Are You an Enabling Parent?" Crosswalk.com, Febrary 3, 2009, http://www.crosswalk.com/family/parenting/when-helping-hurts-are-you-an-enabling-parent-11599054.html.
3. Johannes P. Louw and Eugene Albert Nida, *Greek-English Lexicon of the New Testament: Based on Semantic Domains* (New York: United Bible Societies, 1996), 507.
4. D. A. Carson et al., eds., *New Bible Commentary: 21st Century Edition*, 4th ed. (Leicester, England; Downers Grove, IL: InterVarsity, 1994), 1252.

## CHAPTER TWO: WHY MILLENNIALS ARE LEAVING THE FAITH

1. Norman L. Geisler and Jason Jimenez, *The Bible's Answers to 100 of Life's Biggest Questions* (Grand Rapids, MI: Baker Books, 2015), 271–272.

2. Christian Smith, *Lost in Translation: The Dark Side of Emerging Adulthood* (New York: Oxford University Press, 2011), 11.

3. Cited in "Millennials: Confident. Connected. Open to Change," *Pew Research Center*, February 24, 2010, http://www.pewsocialtrends.org /2010/02/24/millennials-confident-connected-open-to-change/.

4. "Millennials and the Bible: New Study On Millennials and the Bible Tracks Scripture Engagement Trend," American Bible Society, http:// www.americanbible.org/features/millenials-and-the-bible.

5. W. Travis Stewart, "Xanax and the Millennial Generation," Addiction Hope, http://www.addictionhope.com/xanax/xanax-abuse-among-college -students/xanax-and-the-millennial-generation.

6. Chap Clark, *Hurt 2.0: Inside the World of Today's Teenagers*, (Grand Rapids, MI: Baker Academic, 2011), 9.

7. John W. Santrock, *Adolescence*, 8th ed. (New York: McGraw-Hill, 2001), 28–29.

8. Michael J. Bradley, *Yes, Your Teen Is Crazy!: Loving Your Kid without Losing Your Mind* (Gig Harbor, WA: Harbor, 2002), 6–7.

9. Melinda Beck, "Delayed Development: 20-Somethings Blame the Brain," *Wall Street Journal*, August 23, 2012, http://www.wsj.com/articles/SB1000 08723963904437137045776015322208760746.

10. James W. Fowler, *Stages of Faith: The Psychology of Human Development and the Quest for Meaning* (San Francisco: Harper and Row, 1981).

11. Chart developed by Jason Jimenez.

12. Naomi Wolf, "The Porn Myth," *New York Magazine*, http://nymag.com /nymag/features/coverstory/n_9437/.

13. Ken Ham, "The 20s Generation—Lost Christian Worldview and Lost Biblical Foundation," *Answers in Genesis*, August 27, 2015, https://answers ingenesis.org/blogs/ken-ham/2015/08/27/lost-christian-worldview-and -lost-biblical-foundation/.

14. Bradley R. Entner Wright, *Christians Are Hate-Filled Hypocrites—and Other Lies You've Been Told* (Minneapolis, MN: Bethany House, 2010), 66.

15. "Religion Among the Millennials," *Pew Research Center Religion & Public Life RSS*, February 17, 2010, http://www.pewforum.org/2010/02/17 /religion-among-the-millennials/.

## CHAPTER THREE: WHAT LIES BEHIND ABANDONED FAITH

1. "Do Millennial Christians Have the Strongest Faith of Any Generation?" *Relevant* magazine, http://www.relevantmagazine.com/god/god-our -generation/do-Millennial-christians-have-strongest-faith-any -generation/.

2. Alex McFarland, quoted in "5 Freedoms from Christ," *Engage*, November 10, 2015, http://www.engagemagazine.net/worldview /5-freedoms-from-christ/.

## CHAPTER FOUR: HOW THE CHURCH IS FAILING MILLENNIALS (AND HOW IT CAN IMPROVE)

1. Rachel Held Evans, "Why Millennials Are Leaving the Church." *CNN Belief Blog*, July 27, 2013, http://religion.blogs.cnn.com/2013/07/27/why -millennials-are-leaving-the-church/.
2. Bradley R. Entner Wright, *Christians Are Hate-Filled Hypocrites—and Other Lies You've Been Told* (Minneapolis, MN: Bethany House, 2010), 155.
3. Bruce Drake, "6 New findings about Millennials," *Pew Research Center*, March 7, 2014, http://www.pewresearch.org/fact-tank/2014/03/07/6-new -findings-about-Millennials/.
4. Ibid.

## CHAPTER FIVE: STRUGGLES MILLENNIALS FACE

1. "Generation Z Opts to Stash Their Cash in Savings Rather Than Invest," TD Ameritrade, September 11, 2014, http://s1.q4cdn.com/959385532 /files/doc_downloads/research/Gen-Z-and-Money-2014-Research-Report .pdf
2. Abby Stone, "5 Revelations About Millennials and Money, According to Facebook," *Mental Floss*, February 4, 2016, http://mentalfloss.com /article/74928/5-revelations-about-Millennials-and-money-according -facebook.
3. Owen Davis, "Millennials and Their Money: Portrait of a Generation," *International Business Times*, October 1, 2015, http://www.ibtimes.com /Millennials-their-money-portrait-generation-2119516.
4. Charlotte Alter, "Millennials Are Setting New Records—for Living with Their Parents." *Time*, November 11, 2015, http://time.com/4108515 /millennials-live-at-home-parents/.
5. Jen Doll, "How to Just Be a Twentysomething," *The Wire*, August 21, 2012, http://www.thewire.com/entertainment/2012/08/how-just-be -twentysomething/56017/.
6. Cited in "Millennials in Adulthood," *Pew Research Center*, March 7, 2014, http://www.pewsocialtrends.org/2014/03/07/Millennials-in-adulthood/.
7. Jennifer Ludden, "For More Millennials, It's Kids First, Marriage Maybe," NPR, October 16, 2014, http://www.npr.org/2014/10/16/354625221 /for-more-millennials-its-kids-first-marriage-maybe.

**CHAPTER SIX: UNDERSTANDING WHAT DRIVES MILLENNIALS**

1. Fred Dews, "Eleven Facts about the Millennial Generation," *Brookings Now*, June 2, 2014, http://www.brookings.edu/blogs/brookings-now/posts /2014/06/11-facts-about-the-Millennial-generation.

2. Morley Winograd and Michael Hais, "How Millennials Could Upend Wall Street and Corporate America," *Brookings Now*, May 28, 2014, http:// www.brookings.edu/research/papers/2014/05/millenials-upend-wall-street -corporate-america-winograd-hais.

3. Fred Dews, "11 Facts about the Millennial Generation," *Brookings Now*, June 2, 2014, http://www.brookings.edu/blogs/brookings-now/posts/2014 /06/11-facts-about-the-Millennial-generation.

4. "5 Ways to Connect with Millennials," *Barna Releases*, September 9, 2014, https://www.barna.com/research/5-ways-to-connect-with-millennials/.

5. "The Millennial Generation Research Review," US Chamber of Commerce Foundation, 2012, https://www.uschamberfoundation.org/reports /Millennial-generation-research-review.

6. Dan Schawbel, "74 of the Most Interesting Facts about Millennials," blog, June 25, 2013, http://danschawbel.com/blog/74-of-the-most -interesting-facts-about-the-millennial-generation/.

7. Cited in "Millennials: Confident. Connected. Open to Change," *Pew Research Center*, February 24, 2010, http://www.pewsocialtrends.org/2010/02/24 /millennials-confident-connected-open-to-change/.

8. Cited in "Millennial Is a State of Mind, a Survey Commissioned by Zipcar, April 2015," slideshare.net, http://www.slideshare.net/Zipcar_PR /zipcar2015-millennialmind-slideshare/1

9. Daniel Cox, PhD, Robert P. Jones, PhD, Thomas Banchoff, "A Generation in Transition," Public Religion Research Institute, April 19, 2012, http:// publicreligion.org/research/2012/04/Millennial-values-survey-2012.

10. Cited in "Millennials: Confident. Connected. Open to Change," *Pew Research Center*, February 24, 2010, http://www.pewsocialtrends.org /2010/02/24/millennials-confident-connected-open-to-change/.

11. Cox, Jones, Banchoff, "A Generation in Transition."

12. Ibid.

13. "Millennials in Adulthood," *Pew Research Center*, March 7, 2014, http:// www.pewsocialtrends.org/2014/03/07/Millennials-in-adulthood/.

14. Cited in "Millennials: Confident. Connected. Open to Change," *Pew Research Center*, February 24, 2010, http://www.pewsocialtrends.org /2010/02/24/millennials-confident-connected-open-to-change/.

15. "The Millennial Generation Research Review," US Chamber of Commerce Foundation, 2012, https://www.uschamberfoundation.org/reports /Millennial-generation-research-review.
16. Cited in "Millennials: Confident. Connected. Open to Change," *Pew Research Center*, February 24, 2010, http://www.pewsocialtrends.org /2010/02/24/millennials-confident-connected-open-to-change/.

**CHAPTER SEVEN: HOPE FOR A GENERATION**
1. TEDxTalks, "TEDxSF—Scott Hess—Millennials: Who They Are & Why We Hate Them," YouTube.com, June 10, 2011.
2. "Simon Mainwaring." BrainyQuote.com, http://www.brainyquote.com /quotes/authors/s/simon_mainwaring.html.

**CHAPTER EIGHT: STRENGTHENING YOUR RELATIONSHIP IN STRESSFUL TIMES**
1. TD Canada Trust, *TD Canada Trust Savings Poll* (Toronto: Envi-ronics Research Group, 2013).
2. Caroline Beaton, "8 Habits That Make Millennials Stressed, Anxious and Unproductive," *Forbes*, February 18, 2016, http://www.forbes.com /sites/carolinebeaton/2016/02/18/8-habits-that-make-millennials-stressed -anxious-and-unproductive/.

**CHAPTER TEN: HELPING YOUR CHILD BOUNCE BACK FROM TOUGH BREAKS**
1. Laura Petrecca, "Toughest Test Comes after Graduation: Getting a Job," *USA Today*, May 21, 2010, http://usatoday30.usatoday.com/money /economy/employment/2010-05-19-jobs19_CV_N.htm.
2. Alex Kennedy, "Rejecting Hypocrisy and Pursuing Integrity," Carmel Baptist Church, April 11, 2016, http://carmelbaptist.org/media/sermons /rejecting-hypocrisy-and-pursuing-integrity/.
3. Paul David Tripp, *Awe: Why It Matters for Everything We Think, Say, and Do* (Wheaton, IL: Crossway, 2015), 159–160.
4. Paul David Tripp, *Age of Opportunity: A Biblical Guide to Parenting Teens* (Phillipsburg, NJ: P & R, 2001), 16.

**CHAPTER ELEVEN: THE POWER OF PRAYER**
1. Stormie Omartian, *The Power of a Praying Parent* (Eugene, OR: Harvest House, 1995), 12.
2. Edward M. Bounds, *The Necessity of Prayer* (Oak Harbor, WA: Logos Research Systems, 1999).

3. Andrew Murray, *Humility: The Journey Toward Holiness* (Minneapolis, MN: Bethany House, 2001).
4. Thriving Family, *Prayers for Your Kids*, Focus on the Family, 2013.

**CHAPTER TWELVE: BUILD A FOUNDATION OF BIBLICAL TRUTH**
1. Christian Smith and Melinda Lundquist Denton, *Soul Searching: The Religious and Spiritual Live of American Teenagers* (New York: Oxford University Press, 2005), 56.
2. Jim Daly, "Three Things Parents of Adult Children in the Home Should Consider," Focus on the Family, September 4, 2013, http://www.focuson thefamily.com/parenting/adult-parenting/parenting-adult-children/three -things-parents-of-adult-children-in-the-home-should-consider
3. Sean McDowell, *Apologetics for a New Generation* (Eugene, OR: Harvest House, 2009), 61.
4. Paul Little, *Know What You Believe: A Practical Discussion of The Fundamentals of the Christian Faith* (Wheaton, IL: Victor Books, 1987), 27.

**APPENDIX: WHEN THERE'S A FAILURE TO LAUNCH**
1. Kim Abraham and Marney Studaker-Cordner, "Failure to Launch, Part 3," empoweringparents.com, https://www.empoweringparents.com/article /failure-to-launch-part-3-six-steps-to-help-your-adult-child-move-out/.

# ABOUT THE AUTHORS

**ALEX MCFARLAND** is a speaker, writer, and advocate for apologetics who has spoken in hundreds of locations throughout the US and abroad. He has preached in over 1,500 different churches throughout North America and internationally. He has written over 150 published articles and is author of 16 books, including *The Ten Most Common Objections to Christianity, Stand Strong in College*, and three books in the Stand series (Focus on the Family/Tyndale). He has cowritten with Elmer Towns *10 Questions Every Christian Must Answer*. Learn more at his website, AlexMcFarland.com.

Alex cohosts Explore the Word, which is heard weekdays in nearly 200 radio markets, and he cohosts the weekly television program "Viral Truth" with Jason Jimenez on the National Religious Broadcasters network. He is married to Angie McFarland and lives in North Carolina.

**JASON JIMENEZ** is the founder of Stand Strong Ministries. He is a pastor, apologist, and national speaker who has ministered to families since 1998. Jason is the author of several books, including *The Raging War of Ideas*, *The Bible's Answers to 100 of Life's Biggest Questions* with Dr. Norman Geisler, and *Stand Strong America: Courage, Freedom & Hope for Tomorrow* with Dr. Alex McFarland.

Jason travels all over America with the Stand Strong Tour. He and his wife, Celia, live in Charlotte, North Carolina, with their four beautiful children. For more information on his ministry, visit standstrongministries.org.

# Look for these additional parenting resources wherever fine books are sold:

**Plugged-In Parenting**
Parents are looking for ways to protect their children from the increasingly violent and sexualized content of movies, TV, the Internet, and music as well as cyberbullying and obsessive cell phone texting. *Plugged-In Parenting* makes a powerful case for teaching kids media discernment but doesn't stop there. It shows how to use teachable moments, evidence from research and pop culture, Scripture, questions, parental example, and a written family entertainment constitution to uphold biblical standards without damaging the parent-child relationship.

**Losing Control and Liking It**
Parents of teens—especially Christian ones—know only too well that many sons and daughters abandon the "straight and narrow" when they hit adulthood. The pressure on these parents to make their kids turn out right is enormous and can lead parents to think they have to control their kids. *Losing Control and Liking It* offers parents relief of a burden they were never meant to carry and will help build family relationships based on validation and nurturing instead of control.

**TrueU Series**
*Does God Exist? Is the Bible Reliable?* Everyone asks these questions, and maybe you think you have the answers. But can you defend your beliefs when peers and professors are challenging your worldview? In the TrueU series, Dr. Stephen Meyer helps you examine the evidence and provides the tools needed to defend your faith and make it your own.